PRAISE FOR
Spiritual Housecleaning

Hosea says, "My people are destroyed for lack of knowledge" (Hos. 4:6). Alice and Eddie Smith share prophetic and practical truths that will bring greater freedom for you and your family. I highly commend this outstanding book.

DR. CHÉ AHN
PASTOR, HARVEST ROCK CHURCH
PASADENA, CALIFORNIA

Many things in the world today that are called faddish are a fetish. God has opened the eyes of Eddie and Alice Smith's understanding to teach us on how to keep these things out of our homes. Open your hearts to this book's message and enjoy!

KIM DANIELS

This book is a timely message to the Body of Christ, calling us all to a new level of holiness. We have left open spiritual doors to the enemy in our homes, churches and hearts. Alice and Eddie Smith have given us the keys to free ourselves from demonic hindrances that have infiltrated our walk with God.

FRANCIS FRANGIPANE
AUTHOR, *THE THREE BATTLEGROUNDS*
PASTOR, RIVER OF LIFE MINISTRIES
CEDAR RAPIDS, IOWA

The Bible admonishes us to "leave no [such] room or foothold for the devil [give no opportunity to him]" (Eph. 4:27, *AMP*). Eddie and Alice Smith show how, through our ignorance and carelessness, the devil can take advantage of us through things in our possession. From Scripture and personal experience they enlighten us on the importance of *Spiritual Housecleaning* and how to go about it.

FRANK D. HAMMOND
AUTHOR, *PIGS IN THE PARLOR* AND *A PRACTICAL GUIDE TO DELIVERANCE*

Eddie and Alice Smith and their book *Spiritual Housecleaning* have managed to capture with great insight issues that plague many people because of historical and spiritual violations on people's land prior to them purchasing it. This can include their houses. I believe this book to be essential in understanding how spiritual powers work and how to combat those forces and ensure God's presence.

JOHN PAUL JACKSON
STREAMS MINISTRIES INTERNATIONAL

Satan and the forces of evil do everything they can to discourage the Christian—including attempting to invade our homes. This is part of the conflict in the invisible world. We must be aware of and cut off the subtle ways Satan trespasses and attempts to rob us of blessings right where we live. Eddie and Alice Smith point us to the place where we must begin—in our own souls and homes. They show us how to cleanse our attitudes and every physical room where we reside. The Smiths give us a step-by-step guide to taking unlimited authority over demons and reclaiming our homes for the Lord. They show us how to apply the biblical truth that in God's wonderful order, "He who is in you is greater than he who is in the world" (1 John 4:4).

PAT ROBERTSON
HOST, *THE 700 CLUB*
CHAIRMAN AND CEO, THE CHRISTIAN BROADCASTING NETWORK

Spiritual Housecleaning is a practical tool for every believer committed to living a holy and free life! I have personally seen people around the world bring hundreds of items to an altar of repentance to break their ties with sin. I highly recommend this book, as it is written by qualified servants of the Lord, Eddie and Alice Smith, who have accumulated a wealth of experience on the subject for over 30 years. This book is a gift from God to the Body of Christ around the world, offering teaching and instruction on how to finally keep our homes and lives free of any spiritual trash.

SERGIO SCATAGLINI
AUTHOR, *THE FIRE OF HIS HOLINESS*
PRESIDENT, SCATAGLINI MINISTRIES, INC.

If we are ignorant of the wiles of the devil, he will surely take advantage of us. With *Spiritual Housecleaning,* Eddie and Alice Smith have exposed his wiles and dealt a severe blow to the kingdom of darkness. This book will help you break satanic bondages and set you free for victory!

C. PETER WAGNER
CHANCELLOR, WAGNER LEADERSHIP INSTITUTE

SPIRITUAL
HOUSE
CLEANING

ALICE & EDDIE SMITH

Regal

From Gospel Light
Ventura, California, U.S.A.

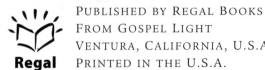

PUBLISHED BY REGAL BOOKS
FROM GOSPEL LIGHT
VENTURA, CALIFORNIA, U.S.A.
Regal   PRINTED IN THE U.S.A.

Regal Books is a ministry of Gospel Light, a Christian publisher dedicated to serving the local church. We believe God's vision for Gospel Light is to provide church leaders with biblical, user-friendly materials that will help them evangelize, disciple and minister to children, youth and families.

It is our prayer that this Regal book will help you discover biblical truth for your own life and help you meet the needs of others. May God richly bless you.

For a free catalog of resources from Regal Books/Gospel Light, please call your Christian supplier or contact us at 1-800-4-GOSPEL *or* www.regalbooks.com.

Cover and interior design by Robert Williams
Edited by Rose Decaen

Library of Congress Cataloging-in-Publication Data
Smith, Alice, 1950-
    Spiritual housecleaning / Alice and Eddie Smith.
        p. cm.
Includes bibliographical references.
    ISBN 0-8307-3107-5
1. Spiritual warfare. I. Title: Spiritual house cleaning. II. Smith,
Eddie. III. Title.
    BV4509.5 .S62 2003
    235'.4—dc21   2002156098

    13 14 15 16 17 18 19 20 / 14 13 12 11 10 09 08

Rights for publishing this book in other languages are contracted by Gospel Light Worldwide, the international nonprofit ministry of Gospel Light. Gospel Light Worldwide also provides publishing and technical assistance to international publishers dedicated to producing Sunday School and Vacation Bible School curricula and books in the languages of the world. For additional information, visit www.gospellightworldwide.org; write to Gospel Light Worldwide, P.O. Box 3875, Ventura, CA 93006; or send an e-mail to info@gospellightworldwide.org.

DISCLAIMER

Please exercise caution and wisdom before destroying antiques, furniture, jewelry and other things that have monetary value. The Holy Spirit should direct everything we do as we spiritually clean our homes. Colossians 3:15 reminds us: "And let the peace of God rule in your hearts."

CONTENTS

WHY WE WROTE THIS BOOK

Imagine there were a plague of snakes of biblical proportion in your city. The house in which you live is completely overrun with deadly, poisonous snakes. How important would it be for you to make sure *some* of the snakes were removed? You wouldn't even consider that an option, would you? Absolutely not! You would insist that *all* of the snakes be removed if you and your family were to continue living there. Could you sleep peacefully if you thought there might be *even one* poisonous snake left in your home? Hardly.

Would you believe there could be possessions inside your home right now that pose a spiritual threat to you and your family like poisonous snakes pose a physical threat? The average

Christian family may not even be aware of the necessity to *spiritually clean* their house in order to experience the peaceful presence of God. That's why we wrote this book.

Many of us are suffering today because we have sometimes willfully, and sometimes ignorantly, invited possessions and behaviors into our homes that defile the atmosphere and give the devil the right to affect our lives and the lives of our children. This defilement can come in many forms: statues of foreign gods, "magic" charms, souvenirs of past sins. But whatever the form, God does not want us possessing defiled objects, for they invite the devil to wreak havoc with our lives and our hearts. That is clearly not how Christ wants us to live. Paul tells us in 1 Corinthians 10:20, "I do not want you to have fellowship with demons."

To the uninitiated reader some of what is contained in this book may sound a bit like superstition. We understand where you are coming from. According to *Webster's* definition of "superstition,"[1] some could even conclude that our belief in a spirit world and faith in an unseen God is a superstition. To us, superstition is placing faith in any person, place or thing other than the almighty God and His infallible Word. We unfold not legalism nor superstition but biblical principles and proven practices that can indeed free us and our households from any spiritual bondage.

That being said, Christ's cross and resurrection have established our authority over the devil. Since Jesus has given us His authority, we are to live on the offensive (see Matt. 10:1; Luke 19:10; Eph. 6:10).

For that reason, we should never fear the devil or demons. Jesus set the example for us when He taught us to pray "deliver us from evil" (Matt. 6:13, *KJV*). The Lord's deliverance is always available to those who walk in the way of righteousness. With this knowledge, as children of the King, we exchange our fear for freedom. Yet to live fully in our inheritance, we must be sure there is nothing in our lives or in our homes that would hinder our fellowship with God.

What does purity of heart entail for us as Christians? What does it mean to love God with heart, soul and mind? It means not allowing Satan access to any aspect of our lives, thereby keeping ourselves free from defilement. It means not giving Satan any place or allowing him any opportunity (see Eph. 4:27).

Today is a new day for the Church! It is time for the Church of Jesus Christ to awaken from her slumber. No longer can we afford to wallow in the carnality of the world and expect the Lord to overlook it. Today God is calling us to a new level of holiness. We need to cleanse the atmosphere of our homes as well as our hearts. This cleansing often involves the removal of certain physical possessions. But which ones?

We have written this book to teach you how to walk circumspectly and to exercise spiritual discernment (see 1 Cor. 2:15; Eph. 5:15). It may very well prove to be one of the most important books you will ever read, because its principles can provide the key to spiritual peace and security for you and your entire family.

We have a world to reach with the gospel! But before we can reach a fallen world, both our lives and homes must reflect God's kingdom rule. We live not under legalism or the tyranny of performance but in the purity that flows from grateful hearts that know we owe everything to our Lord and Savior, Jesus Christ!

Note

1. *Merriam-Webster's Collegiate Dictionary*, 10th ed., s.v. "superstition."

SPIRITUAL DISCERNMENT

The woman's voice on the other end of the line sounded eerie and mystical. She had sought help from a Christian psychiatric hospital that had referred her to us. This divorced woman and her eight-year-old daughter lived alone, trapped in a world of darkness. The small girl's father was a Unitarian pastor; but prior to that he had been an African witch doctor in a tribe known as the Leopard People. The now-abandoned single mom had extensive knowledge of the occult; and although she testified to having been recently born again, torment still lived inside the walls of her home.

At her request, we visited her home. Cats fearfully scurried from under our feet as our small prayer team approached the apartment door. When the attractive woman opened the door, we were introduced to an atmosphere that almost took our breath away—it felt electric with evil.

Once inside, two large cats cowering near the refrigerator hissed at us, then disappeared within seconds. The electrical power began to flash off and on until we commanded it to stop. To the right of the front door was a 10-foot bookcase filled with religious, heathen and occult books. After we had been invited to sit down we began to discuss her problems.

She explained that her daughter was being harassed in the night by nightmares and apparitions. The child would awaken to see ghosts in her room. (The ghosts actually were demons appearing in the forms of an old African-aboriginal man and woman.) The concerned mother stated that at times the child would leap on top of the dressers and move about like a leopard. This precious little girl would sometimes wake in the morning with humanlike bite marks and claw scratches in the middle of her back. One night, the frightened girl awakened her mother several times, complaining that the flies had bitten her. Each time her mother turned on the lights and searched the room but found nothing. The next morning when she opened the window shades, she found a mound of dead flies piled on her daughter's windowsill. This did not surprise us—we know that Satan is sometimes spoken of as Beelzebub, the lord of the flies (see Matt. 12:24-32; Mark 3:22).

It was clear that the enemy had been given authority to operate in this home. As we prayed and asked God for wisdom and discernment, we waited for the Holy Spirit's direction. At times the demonic reality was almost palpable. Spiritual impressions from the Lord (i.e. "the word of knowledge" [1 Cor. 12:8]) came to our team members as we cleansed the atmosphere with prayer. All at once, as though the team were acting on the same inspiration, we stared at the wall of books—her huge library on the occult. We explained to the young mother that the books and the artwork were acting as bait for the demons. (As flies are attracted to dung, demons are attracted to darkness.) Her library was an open invitation that attracted demonic spirits and gave them legal right to defile her home and harass her and her child. These books were like a welcome mat to the unseen demonic world, communicating that they had the woman's permission to stay. Such items and artifacts may seem harmless, yet hold significance to satanic spirits.

We urgently appealed to the mother that she discard the books, even offering to help her get rid of them. She refused. She lamented about the money she had invested in the books. We begged her for the sake of her daughter to spiritually clean the house, but she turned a deaf ear to us. Sadly, we were unable to go any further. We lovingly explained that we had no authority to help her because of her unwillingness to remove the ungodly books. Our insight as to why the child was harassed involved the occult materials and her mother's unhealthy attachment to them. These occult materials were also symbols of contracts the mother had made with the enemy.

We need only look to C. Peter Wagner's account of the power of idols in the ancient city of Athens to see why this woman's attachment to her library served as a welcoming gesture to the devil.

The only place in the Bible where we find the phrase "given over to idols" (from the Greek *kateidolos*) is where Luke describes Athens in Acts 17:16. Athens was the idol capital of the ancient world, possibly comparable to Kyoto, Japan, today. The literature of that day describes Athens as a forest of idols in which it is easier to find a god than a human being. Certain streets had so many idols that pedestrian traffic was difficult. One observer estimated that Athens contained more idols than the rest of Greece combined!

Because idols themselves are only made of wood or stone or metal, some are not concerned about their presence. These idols, however, were not just any piece of wood or stone or metal. They had been carefully and intentionally crafted by human beings as forms in the visible world through which the forces of the invisible world of darkness were invited to control the lives of people, families and the city as a whole, locking the people in spiritual darkness. That's why we read that Paul's "spirit was provoked within him" (v. 16).[1]

Yet this is not the only and perhaps not the most significant illustration of defilement. Let's look at what happened to Joshua in the Old Testament. (The following is a loose adaptation of Joshua 7; the fictional character named Elisiaph has been added to the account.)

A PIECE OF CAKE?

"Now sir, let's not overreact," suggested Elisiaph, General Joshua's senior military adviser. "We can relax now and give the men a break. Trust me—this one is going to be a piece of cake. According to our reconnaissance, there's no reason at all for you to send the entire Israeli army to attack such a small place as Ai. ["Ai" literally means "a heap of ruin."] I suggest that a reduced force of 2,000 or 3,000 troops will be sufficient to utterly destroy the city."

So the next morning Joshua sent 3,000 troops to annihilate Ai. To their surprise, the men of Ai were ready for battle. The feisty troops of Ai killed 36 Israeli soldiers and chased the others from the gate of the city down the slope to the stone quarries. The dispirited Israeli army was forced to retreat like a dog with its tail tucked between its legs.

Joshua was stunned when he heard the news. The Israelites had only recently defeated the big city of Jericho, which now lay in smoldering ruins. *How could Elisiaph have so grossly underestimated the military capability of a small town like Ai?* Joshua wondered. *More important—where was God? And what about the promises He had made to them?* God had clearly said,

> Joshua, I am giving to you the land I promised Moses. I will always be with you and I will help you as I helped him. No one will ever be able to defeat you. So be strong and courageous! Do everything Moses taught you. Never stop reading the Book of the Law he gave you. Think about what it says day and night. Obey it completely and you will be able to take this land (see Josh. 1:1-9).

Joshua called together an emergency council meeting of Israel's leaders. "Gentlemen," he said, "you will recall that Jehovah God promised us that He would never leave us and that we would never be defeated. Where do you suppose we went wrong when that handful of untrained, ragtag men disgraced our troops today? May I suggest, sirs, that we have a national emergency on our hands? And we must get to the bottom of this—*now!*"

So Joshua and the leaders tore their clothes and put dirt on their heads as a symbol of sorrow and repentance. They lay facedown on the ground in front of the Ark of the Covenant and cried out to God until sunset.

Then Joshua prayed:

> Lord, did you bring us across the Jordan just so the Amorites could annihilate us? If we had stayed on the other side of the Jordan, none of this would have happened. Frankly, I'm speechless. It is shocking to realize that our army actually ran from their enemy today. Our people are beginning to think that You can no longer protect us. When our enemies hear of our humiliation,

they are likely to become emboldened. They may even try to surround us and wipe us out.

The Lord answered Joshua:

General, get up off your face! I'm not taking prayer requests at this time. I told you that everything in Jericho belonged to me. Furthermore, I told you that I wanted the entire city to be destroyed. But instead, your people have stolen and hidden some of the booty for yourselves; and you've lied about it.

Because you've stolen stuff that was supposed to be destroyed, Israel itself has been set aside for destruction. I can't help you anymore until you do exactly what I've told you to do. And that's precisely why your army could not stand before its enemies today.

Tell the people that they'll never be able to stand against another enemy until they rid themselves of the abominable things that they've hidden. Tell them to prepare for worship. Tomorrow morning, when they gather for worship, I will identify for you the guilty tribe and point out the guilty clan and the guilty family. And I will show you the man who has stolen the forbidden things that have defiled Israel and have broken the sacred covenant I have made with you. That man, along with his wife, his sons and his daughters, must be executed by stoning. Their bodies and all of their possessions must be burned.

Early the next morning Joshua brought each tribe to the place of worship. There the Lord identified Judah as the guilty tribe and the clan of Zerah and Zabdi's family as the guilty clan and family. He showed them that Achan was the man responsible for violating Israel's contract with God.

General Joshua said, "Achan, is it true? Don't try to hide anything from me. Tell me what you've done."

"Yes, sir, it's true," Achan answered reluctantly. "I'm the one who sinned against the Lord God of Israel. While we were mopping up at Jericho, I found a beautiful Babylonian robe, 200 pieces of silver and a gold bar that weighed as much as 50 pieces of gold. I wanted them for myself, so I took and hid them in a hole beneath my tent."

So Joshua immediately sent men running to Achan's tent to retrieve the silver, the gold and the robe. They brought the defiled items back and laid them before the Lord so that Joshua and the rest of the Israelites could see them.

Then everyone took Achan, his sons and daughters, his cattle, donkeys, and sheep, his tent and everything that belonged to him, as well as the things he had stolen, to a nearby valley.

Once there, Joshua said, "Achan, you've caused us a lot of trouble. Now you are in trouble."

The people of Israel stoned Achan, his family and his animals to death. They built a fire and burned the bodies, along with all the possessions and the cursed things that Achan had stolen. They covered the ashes with a big pile of rocks. And that place is still known as Trouble Valley.[2]

Then God stopped being angry with Israel and gave them the city of Ai (see Josh. 8:1).

TEN LESSONS WE LEARN FROM THIS ACCOUNT

1. God's Promises to Us Are Awesome!

Our great God is a promise-keeping God. He has literally given us thousands of promises in His Word. Salvation is only the beginning of God's promises. Beyond our salvation experience there are countless treasures waiting for us to experience in Christ, because God "has blessed us with every spiritual blessing in the heavenly places in Christ" (Eph. 1:3). Furthermore,

> We have everything we need to live a life that pleases God. It was all given to us by God's own power, when we learned that he had invited us to share in his wonderful goodness. God made great and marvelous promises, so that his nature would become part of us. Then we could escape our evil desires and the corrupt influences of this world (2 Pet. 1:3-4, *CEV*).

Have you realized that once you are born again, His nature becomes part of you?

2. God's Promises Are Often Contingent upon Our Obedience

In order for us to enjoy the benefits that God has promised, we must trust Him and believe that He keeps His Word. His promises are activated by our faith. However, many of God's promises are conditional. They are contingent upon our obedience. We call them God's If/Then promises.

With regard to our salvation, He's promised that "if" we believe in our hearts and "if" we confess with our mouths, we shall be saved (see Rom. 10:9).

With regard to His forgiveness of our sins, He has promised that "If we confess our sins, He is faithful and just to forgive us our sins and to cleanse us from all unrighteousness" (1 John 1:9).

God had made covenant with Joshua and had given him promises too. He promised to give him the land He had promised Moses (see Josh. 1:1-4,15); to always be with him and to help him, as He had helped Moses (see Josh. 1:9); that he would never be defeated (see Josh. 1:5)

But with those three promises, there were three commands, or conditions: be strong and courageous (see Josh. 1:6); do everything Moses taught (see Josh. 1:7); read, meditate on and obey the Book of the Law (see Josh. 1:8).

Achan had failed to do everything God had asked of him. He had taken that which God had specifically forbidden the Israelites to take—things that God had designated for destruction—and he had hidden the goods in a hole in the ground beneath his tent. Although the Lord doesn't indicate that a demonic power was attached to the Babylonian garment, the 200 pieces of silver or the 50 gold shekels, God said these things were accursed and should be avoided. Why would God want the Israelites to avoid these things—unless they brought evil with them?

Physical things can carry spiritual significance.

Therefore, the main idea of the biblical passages dealing with this subject is that disobedience to Yahweh brings a curse. Such disobedience is inherent in the worship of alien gods (idolatry), which is in fact the worship of demons, according to the Old Testament (see Deut. 32:16-18).

3. Physical Things Sometimes Carry Spiritual Significance

Throughout Scripture we see evidence that physical things can carry spiritual significance: the lamb's blood that God had the children of Israel apply to their doorposts (see Exod. 12:7-13); the Tabernacle, its furnishings and utensils (see Exod. 26—27); water baptism (see Luke 3:21-22); the Last Supper (see Matt. 26:28; 1 Cor. 11:23-25); miraculous handkerchiefs and aprons (see Acts 19:11-12); healing oil (see Jas. 5:14). But perhaps the clearest example is found in the Old Testament and is one we're all familiar with—Moses' brass serpent:

> And the people spoke against God and against Moses: "Why have you brought us up out of Egypt to die in the wilderness? For there is no food and no water, and our soul loathes this worthless bread." So the LORD sent fiery serpents among the people, and they bit the people; and many of the people of Israel died. Therefore the people came to Moses, and said, "We have sinned, for we have spoken against the LORD and against you; pray to the LORD that He take away the serpents from us." So Moses prayed for the people. Then the LORD said to Moses, "Make a fiery serpent, and set it on a pole; and it shall be that everyone who is bitten, when he looks at it, shall live." So Moses made a bronze serpent, and put it upon a pole; and so it was, if a serpent had bitten anyone, when he looked at the bronze serpent, he lived (Num. 21:5-9).

The brass serpent that God instructed Moses to elevate on a pole for the children of Israel to see offered a solution for their sin. True, it was only a brass serpent on a pole—an inanimate object; yet it carried healing power to those who were bitten by the poisonous snakes. If they looked upon the brass serpent, they were healed. Today we understand even more about the significance of that brass snake—it symbolized Christ's becoming sin for us when He was lifted upon the Cross as our atoning sacrifice.

Nine hundred years later, when King Hezekiah was cleansing the Temple, "He removed the high places and broke the sacred pillars, cut down the wooden image [Asherah] and *broke in pieces the bronze serpent which Moses had made; for until those days the children of Israel burned incense to it"* (2 Kings 18:4, emphasis added).

Amazingly, after all those years, an object that God had designed for Israel's healing had become a god they worshiped!

While physical things can have a divine significance, they can also carry demonic designs. This is a reality we experienced firsthand at the 1996 International Conference on Prayer and Spiritual Warfare in Charlotte, North Carolina. After teaching at the conference, we were looking for a room where we could do individual counseling. As we opened the door to a small room backstage, we saw pieces of dog feces laid out in the shape of a cross in the center of the floor, pointed toward the pulpit in the adjoining room. A witch had placed them there to curse the meetings that were to begin that evening. Witches believe that physical items provide a point of contact for use by demonic spirits. So their use of fetishes[3] is a common ploy for deception and control.

It's not time to be flaky or superstitious, but it is time to learn how to walk circumspectly with spiritual discernment.

It's not time to be flaky or superstitious, but it is time to learn how to walk circumspectly with spiritual discernment.

To the uninitiated reader, some of the things in this book may sound a bit like superstition. We understand where you are coming from. According to our culture's definition of "superstition," some people could conclude that our belief in a spirit world and faith in an unseen God is a superstition. To us, superstition is placing faith in any person, place or thing other than the almighty God and His infallible Word.

4. There Are Certain Things That We Are Forbidden to Possess

Certain things are inappropriate for God's children to possess. When God saved us, He didn't patch up our old lives; He made us new creations! Paul wrote, "Therefore, if anyone is in Christ, he is a new creation; old things have passed away; behold, all things have become new" (2 Cor. 5:17). Because of our new life in Christ, God expects from us new living as well. We are to put off the old and put on the new. Ephesians 5:8-11 says,

> For you were once darkness, but now you are light in the Lord. Walk as children of light (for the fruit of the [light] is in all *goodness, righteousness,* and *truth*), finding out what is acceptable to the Lord. And have no fellowship with the fruitless works of darkness, but rather expose them (emphasis added).

In Exodus 20:3, God forbade the children of Israel to have any other gods. He is a jealous God—jealous of our trust (see Deut. 4:24; 5:9). In Deuteronomy 18:9-13, God forbade them to engage in witchcraft and astrology. He explained that such activities are an abomination to Him:

> When thou art come into the land which the LORD thy God giveth thee, thou shalt not learn to do after the abominations of those nations. There shall not be found among you any one that maketh his son or his daughter to pass through the fire, or that useth divination, or an observer of times, or an enchanter, or a witch, or a

charmer, or a consulter with familiar spirits, or a wizard, or a necromancer. For all that do these things are an abomination unto the LORD: and because of these abominations the LORD thy God doth drive them out from before thee. Thou shalt be perfect with the LORD thy God (*KJV*).

In the Old Testament we see lists of things that dishonor God and should not be found among His people. These things suggest that there are other gods, which violates the first four commandments.

Take careful heed to yourselves, for you saw no form when the LORD spoke to you at Horeb out of the midst of the fire, lest you act corruptly and make for yourselves a carved image in the form of any figure: the likeness of male or female, the likeness of any animal that is on the earth or the likeness of any winged bird that flies in the air, the likeness of anything that creeps on the ground or the likeness of any fish that is in the water beneath the earth. And take heed, lest you lift your eyes to heaven, and when you see the sun, the moon, and the stars, all the host of heaven, you feel driven to worship them and serve them, which the LORD your God has given to all the peoples under the whole heaven as a heritage. Take heed to yourselves, lest you forget the covenant of the LORD your God which He made with you, and make for yourselves a carved image in the form of anything which the LORD your God has forbidden you. For the LORD your God is a consuming fire, a jealous God (Deut. 4:15-19,23-24).

This list is still valid today. The Father is grieved if we possess statues of other gods—or any objects that seek to gain spiritual power from any source other than the one true God. Such objects are strictly forbidden, because they open the door to supernatural deception, turn people away from God and hinder people's spiritual and physical health.

5. The Use of an Item Can Establish Its Spiritual Significance

Most objects in this world are neither good nor evil in and of themselves. However, the use to which they are put can establish their spiritual significance.

One day we wandered into an idol shop in Madras, India. We were souvenir shopping before leaving to go to the airport. There on an elevated platform sat an artisan holding a log with his bare feet as he skillfully carved it with hammer and chisel.

"What are you making?" we asked the man.

"I'm carving a god," he replied.

"And which god are you carving?"

"I'm carving [he named the Hindu god], our god of prosperity," he answered.

To the artisan's amazement, Eddie aggressively lurched toward him and shouted, "Hurry! Finish it! Quickly . . . quickly!"

"Why? What's the rush?" the man asked with a puzzled expression.

Still animated, Eddie said, "Sir, look out the windows of your shop. Your streets and sidewalks are littered with lepers and beggars. Your people are malnourished and starving. Finish this 'god of prosperity' and get him into the streets so he can do what he's supposed to do!"

We'll never forget the expression on the artisan's face at that moment. It seemed to say, "You know, what you just said makes a lot of sense."

There certainly was nothing wrong with the log the man was holding. But when carved into an object of heathen worship, it carried no efficacy to solve people's poverty, yet it did have spiritual significance that was contrary to the kingdom of God (see Deut. 4:15-19,23-24). Indeed, our more than 30 years of experience with deliverance ministry has convinced us that demons sometimes attach themselves to certain places and objects, just as they attach themselves to people.

Referring to man-made idols, Paul said, "We know that *an idol is nothing* in the world, and that there is no other God but one" (1 Cor. 8:4, emphasis added). So in and of themselves idols are simply powerless objects, and the meat sacrificed to them is nothing more than meat.

However, Paul went on to explain, "What am I saying then? That an idol is anything, or what is offered to idols is anything? Rather, that the things which the Gentiles sacrifice they sacrifice to demons and not to God, and I do not want you to have fellowship with demons" (1 Cor. 10:19-20).[4]

The idols they worship can become tools of the devil; and even their own lives are then open to demonic influence.

Inanimate objects, crafted by human hands, have been used to commune with demons. The spiritual strength behind the idol is demonic. The demons use the idol to receive worship from people who are deceived and desperate enough to worship them. When they worship the idols, they are wittingly or unwittingly worshiping demons. As a result, the idols they worship can become tools of the devil; and even their own lives are then open to demonic influence. An idol (a statue of a god or goddess) may hold no intrinsic spiritual power, but a demon *is* something! So we can say that through demonic deception people can be led astray indirectly *by* (for example, through the mediation of) these objects.

You might ask why Paul had no problem eating meat that had been offered to idols. His only reluctance to do so was that he would not offend a weaker brother (see 1 Cor. 8:3-13). Wouldn't the meat, a physical object, be subject to a demonic attachment as well?

Of course we don't know for certain. But perhaps food is a special case, since it is created by God to satisfy a universal need. To the contrary, objects that have only one purpose—to operate outside of the governance of God's laws, and to actively and independently work against Him—call for either deliverance or destruction.

A good example of such an instance relates to the day a cable movie channel mysteriously appeared on our television. We called the cable company and said, "Ma'am, we are receiving HBO on our television and we didn't order it."

"That's okay," the lady answered politely.

"No, it's not okay," we insisted. "Let us speak to your general manager."

The general manager came to the phone and said, "Folks, I was told about your call. Don't you worry, we're not going to charge you for the HBO."

"You're not going to charge us?!" we responded hotly. "Sir, you had better hope that we don't charge you! We don't let the city of Houston dump their garbage in our front yard, and we're not about to allow you to dump your 'garbage' in our living room!"

It's amazing how fast that movie channel disappeared!

6. Illicit Possessions Can Separate Us from God's Purposes, His Protection and His Power

God's protection of us and His power released through us are directly related to His purposes for us. When we willfully—or ignorantly for that matter—step away from God's purposes for our lives, we step out from under His protective care.

You can clearly see this in the life of Samson. He forsook God's call on his life to live the life of a fool. Then one day Delilah awoke him: "And she said, 'The Philistines are upon you, Samson!' So he awoke from his sleep, and said, 'I will go out as before, at other times, and shake myself free!' But he did not know that *the LORD had departed from him*" (Judg. 16:20, emphasis added).

It's not that God refused to protect Samson. Samson, in his arrogance and ignorance, forsook God's purpose; and when he did, Samson ceded God's protection and power. Do you agree? Do you see how deception in our lives keeps us from God's wonderful plan for our future?

7. One Person's Crime Can Create Corporate Guilt and Result in Corporate Consequences

We learn an amazing lesson in this case of Joshua and the nation of Israel (see Josh. 7). Only one person—Achan—had sinned; yet God held the whole nation accountable! Look at these plural references (emphasis added) in what God said to Joshua:

> *Israel* (the entire nation) committed a trespass (see Josh. 7:1).
> The anger of the Lord was kindled against *the children of Israel* (all of them) (see v. 1).
> *Israel* sinned (see Josh. 7:11.)
> *Israel* transgressed God's covenant (see v. 11).
> *Israel* took the accursed things (see v. 11).
> *Israel* stole (see v. 11).
> *Israel* put the stolen items among their own things (see v. 11).
> Therefore *the children of Israel* could not stand before *their* enemies (see Josh. 7:12).

They turned *their* backs before *their* enemies, because *they were accursed* (see v. 12).
Neither would God be with *them* any more, unless they destroyed the accursed from among *them* (see v. 12).

Incredibly, one man's sin brought repercussions upon the entire nation. Achan's sin produced corporate consequences. As a result of his sin, 36 soldiers (husbands, sons and fathers) needlessly died in the first futile battle against Ai. As a consequence of Achan's sin, an entire nation was left defenseless and fearful. And in some ways this is the saddest of all: Achan's family—his wife, his sons and daughters, who as far as we know were innocent—were executed along with him.

We also see corporate guilt, as well as redemption, as a New Testament principle. In Romans 5:19, we read, "For as by one man's disobedience many were made sinners, so also by one Man's obedience many will be made righteous."

This corporate nature of the Christian life is somewhat foreign to us as Americans—we typically pride ourselves on our *independence*. We have yet to learn that as members of Christ's Body, we were designed by God not to be independent but rather to be *interdependent* upon each other. And as Paul wrote, "If one part of our body hurts, we hurt all over" (1 Cor. 12:26, *CEV*).

So sir, if you are a Christian man with hidden pornography in your home . . . or ma'am, if you are a Christian lady addicted to soap operas and romance novels, you're very likely spiritually crippling Christ's Church.

8. When We Seek God He Will Reveal the Defiled Things

How can we know which of our possessions dishonor the Lord? Thankfully, we don't have to guess about these things. God has given us His Spirit. Jesus promised, "However, when He, the Spirit of truth, has come, He will guide you into all truth" (John

16:13). When we pursue purity before the Father and ask Him, He will show us if any of our possessions are displeasing to Him. The truth is, God reveals in order to heal!

> When we pursue purity before the Father and ask Him, He will show us if any of our possessions are displeasing to Him.

We experienced just such a healing after God revealed the unseen intruder who invaded our peaceful home at times. We loved our home nestled in the woods far from the busy traffic and hurried lifestyles of Houston, our nation's fourth largest city; but an evil presence (and sometimes odor) would appear in a particular corner of our large family room. We could sense it, and our children often complained when sitting in that part of the room.

One night, as we were pacing the room in prayer for special church services that were to begin later that night, we sensed that evil presence again. Enough was enough! We fervently sought the Lord's revelation as to why! Unwilling to wait any longer, we closely checked all the trinkets and magazines near the corner of the room. When we examined the fireplace mantle, our gaze settled on a beautifully bound, six-volume set of books. We had inherited the elegant collection from a deceased aunt. We had never opened them—they simply were ornaments to grace our mantle. Inside the books were pages filled with lithographs of ghosts, gargoyles and graveyards with spirits ascending from the tombstones. We were appalled! After repenting to the Lord for allowing these books into our home, we spoke aloud, breaking any contracts with demons who were using the books as an access point into our home. Into the trash went those books. The problem never recurred.

Thankfully, because Christ has already died in our place, unlike Achan and his family who died for having the accursed things, you and I will not be executed. Hallelujah! But as the believers in Acts 19 did, we need to rid ourselves of anything that defiles our lives and our homes. We'll talk more (in chapter 4) about what those things might be.

9. We Should Ruthlessly Rid Ourselves of Wicked Things

In his self-indulgence, Achan had abused God's grace and presumed upon God's promises. The result was a welcomed victory to the Canaanites. But as a consequence of their unexpected loss, Israel was awakened, reformed and reconciled to God.

God tells us, "Now these things [Old Testament accounts] became our examples, to the intent that we should not lust after evil things as they also lusted" (1 Cor. 10:6). Having read this experience of Joshua and the children of Israel, we should not have to be forced to allow God to inspect our hearts and our possessions.

In the New Testament we read about a revival in the city of Ephesus.

> Many who had believed came confessing and telling their deeds. Also, many of those who had practiced magic brought their books together and burned them in the sight of all. And they counted up the value of them, and it totaled fifty thousand pieces of silver. So the word of the Lord grew mightily and prevailed (Acts 19:18-20).

Our friend C. Peter Wagner states that the value of the occult items the Ephesians destroyed that day was approximately 4 million U.S. dollars!

God is about the work of His kingdom. And "the kingdom of God is not meat and drink; but righteousness, and peace, and joy in the Holy Ghost" (Rom. 14:17, *KJV*). Our possessions should express the righteousness, peace and joy of God's kingdom. If they don't, the moment the Lord reveals spiritual contamination to us, we should repent and be unrelenting in our commitment to rid ourselves of it for Christ's sake.

Such a vigilant course of action may seem unnecessary—but perhaps you can learn something from Jim, a new believer who had left behind a life of sin and now was passionate about Jesus, his new Messiah! When Jim heard the teaching of spiritual housecleaning, he remembered that his Rolex watch had been a gift from a woman with whom he had lived in adultery. Jim desired to please the Lord. So early the next morning he drove to the city lake, stepped out of his Cadillac, removed the gold and diamond-encrusted watch and threw it as far as he could into the murky water. Later that day he told us about his experience.

"Why did you throw the watch away?" we asked him.

"Because it was symbolic of the unholy relationship I experienced with that woman," he replied.

The watch was more than a watch. To Jim it represented an evil contract that sealed the covenant of sin he had with the woman. However, the watch wasn't inherently evil. It wasn't a golden dragon or designed as a snarling serpent. It was only a very expensive gold watch. Although Jim could have prayed over it, repented for the sin it represented, broken the contracts that it symbolized and sanctified it to the Lord, he opted to destroy it. Had he asked for our counsel, in that case we would have encouraged him to sell the watch and invest the money in the kingdom of God as a gift to his church or to the poor. Let wisdom prevail!

But the point is this: Never underestimate the wiles of the devil—he will explore every option and examine every possible entryway to your life!

10. Obedience Restores Our Fellowship with God and Reinstates His Purposes

As it was with Joshua and the children of Israel, personal cleansing will restore God's presence, reinstate His protection and reignite His power in our lives. (Read in Joshua 8 how the Lord delivered the city of Ai into the hands of the children of Israel.)

PRAYER ASSIGNMENT

Father, in the precious name of Jesus, I am so blessed that You love me enough to show me the truth about my life, my home, my children and possessions. Lord, I don't want to be like Achan who kept a thing that You called defiled. Would You right now, holy God, reveal to me anything with which I need to deal? I desire holiness, and You are holy; so show me the unholy actions in my life or the unholy possessions in my care or the unholy covenants I have made.
In Jesus' name I pray. Amen.

Notes

1. C. Peter Wagner, *Confronting the Powers* (Ventura, CA: Regal Books, 1996), pp. 204-205.
2. A loose adaptation of Joshua 7; General Elisiaph is a character created for the sake of readability.
3. A fetish is an object witches use to vex the environment with magic powers; an amulet is a charm to ward off disease or evil spells.
4. See also Deuteronomy 32:17.

C H A P T E R   T W O

WHO WANTS TO LIVE IN A HAUNTED HOTEL?

More and more television shows are being produced that involve the supernatural. Still, most Americans would assume that haunted houses, for instance, are a thing out of Hollywood movies and Stephen King novels. Others attribute them to an overactive imagination. As a preteen, I (Eddie) remember my older cousin Bill turning off the lights to tell us about the haunted house on the hill above his parents' home. Of course, he always waited until dark to tell the story, but he never persuaded me to go with him to check it out.

Today Alice and I firmly believe in haunted houses, haunted church buildings—even haunted hotels!

One evening in 1990, we received a call from the chief of security at one of Houston's major hotels. The chief was a retired 20-year veteran police officer. He told us this amazing story.

"Two weeks ago a Haitian voodoo conference was held in our hotel. The group was comprised of 100 or so men and women all dressed in white. They rented several rooms at the hotel and used our main ballroom to conduct their ceremonies. Though we thought it a bit bizarre, they stationed their own security guards at the entrances of the ballroom. These huge men would not allow anyone, including my officers and me, near the proceedings.

"One of my security officers inadvertently ventured into the ballroom one night through one of the dining-room service doors. He found the room pitch dark except for candlelight. In the midst of the room sat a man chained in a chair. The worshipers were in a trance, and a bloody ceremony was taking place. He said that it so frightened him that he slammed the door, ran downstairs, jumped into his car and drove home.

"Since that time," our friend went on to say, "our hotel has experienced unusual problems. We have had an abnormal number of thefts from the rooms; arguments and even fistfights among the employees; inexplicable car accidents in front of the hotel; and workers calling in sick in record numbers. The hotel organization is in shambles. Furthermore, all of the employees— including me—are afraid to enter the ballroom where the voodoo ceremonies took place."

He continued, "Tonight, as I drove home from work around the 610 Loop and out Highway 290, I was so frightened that I would get involved in an accident that I drove 15 miles per hour on the shoulder of the road. When I arrived home, my wife suggested that I needed some exercise to relieve my stress. As I began jogging my usual neighborhood route, every time a car came up behind me, I would grimace and my body would get tense. In my imagination I could almost feel a bullet sear its way through my body. I just knew I was going to be shot. I'm calling because someone told my wife that you might be able to help me."

"How long does it take to get to the hotel?" we asked.

"Thirty minutes," he replied.

"Great, we'll meet you there in 30 minutes."

Upon arrival at the hotel, we met the nervous security chief in the lobby and the three of us took the elevator to the fifth floor where the main ballroom was located. While we walked over to the entrance to the ballroom, the security chief stood stiffly to the left of the elevator doors, not willing to move an inch. From a distance, he threw the keys to us. We opened the door and stepped into the dark cavernous room.

The light switches, we discovered, were on the back wall at least 100 feet away. We walked the length of the long, dark room. The atmosphere was oppressive. It was as if the room were filled with a million angry, invisible hornets swarming around us. The air felt electric as waves of spiritual energy pushed past and swept over us. The enemy was desperately trying to frighten us away.

Quietly yet confidently we began to pray. As Nehemiah repented on behalf of others (see Neh. 1:6), we repented to God for what had happened in that room just days before; we asked God to remove the defilement. Then with authority we told the evil spirits to leave. Suddenly, it was as if the tide of spiritual darkness rolled out. The demons departed, and soon the room felt pure and clean. Even the security chief felt safe enough to enter the ballroom.

A week later he called to thank us, reporting that the thefts, the fights, the accidents and the illnesses were gone. He said, "Inexplicably the morning after you prayed through the ballroom, a Bible study was formed in the employee lounge."

SPIRITUAL ATMOSPHERE

Today increasing numbers of Christians are taking a second look at the spiritual environment in their homes. They want their homes, as well as their lives, to reflect the presence of Christ, but this is not often their experience.

As we've searched to find the reasons why, we have discerned three things that contribute to the atmosphere in a home: the attitudes and behavior of the family members who live there, the possessions stored there and the predominant spiritual presence.

Attitudes and Behavior

Our attitudes and behaviors set a table for either a demonic presence or the Holy Spirit's presence. In particular, bad attitudes and bad behavior on the part of parents definitely have an adverse effect on the atmosphere of the home, thus negatively impacting both spouses and children. We need only look to an example from nature to see how parents set the tone for home life:

> The first month of a nightingale's life determines its fate. I had always thought that a nightingale's incomparable song was instinctive and inherited. But it is not so.
>
> Nightingales, to be used as pets, are taken as fledglings from nests of wild birds in the spring. As soon as they lose their fear and accept food, a "master bird" is borrowed that daily sings its lovely song, and the infant bird listens for a period of about a month. This is the way the master bird trains the little wild bird.
>
> If it has a good teacher, the infant bird will learn from experience to produce as beautiful tones as its teacher. But if an infant bird is brought to such a teacher after being raised by wild nightingales, there is always failure, as long experience has shown.

The illustration of the nightingales reminds me that many children's problems could be solved if they just had parents who were "good singers"—parents who take responsibility for the mood or emotional tone of the home—parents who understand that their children are absorbing the emotional atmosphere and learning to respond to life as their moms and dads did.[1]

Each of us must take the responsibility for our sin and its effect upon our spouses and our children. We shouldn't blame the devil for what we ourselves choose to do. When we blow it, we should repent—repentance keeps us close to the Lord and prevents the devil from gaining a foothold in our lives.

Repentance keeps us close to the Lord and prevents the devil from gaining a foothold in our lives.

Is it easy to keep a positive spiritual atmosphere in the home? Of course not. You have to implore the peace of the Holy Spirit to descend upon your home. Then you have to make an effort to cooperate with the Spirit's will for you and your family.

When anger is the rule in a person's life, spirits of anger, hate, malice, resentment, bitterness, jealousy, rage and the like are drawn to them like flies are drawn to honey. When love, joy and peace rule a person's life, demons are repelled and God is blessed. The Holy Spirit is at home in the presence of these Kingdom attributes. In fact, He inhabits the praise of His people! (see Ps. 22:3).

Our Possessions

As surely as bad attitudes and bad behavior adversely affect the spiritual atmosphere of our homes, so do our possessions. What do we mean?

If we were to warn you that to leave certain things around your house would attract deadly snakes, would you leave those things lying around? Of course you wouldn't! Yet having unholy things among our possessions both dishonors God and attracts demons.

In the Old Testament God warned His people to tear down the Asherah poles, dismantle heathen altars and destroy idols (see Judg. 6:25-26). They were to have nothing among their possessions that dishonored God. In the New Testament the newly saved Ephesians were led to burn the books that related to the gods and goddesses of their former religions (see Acts 19:19).

When considering these passages, it's important to remember that our possessions reflect our priorities. They testify of our true spiritual condition. Never did this truth hit home more convincingly than while we were traveling as itinerant evangelists.

During that time we lived in seven different motor homes and travel trailers. Once, while shopping for a new travel trailer, we went to see one that had belonged to a couple who, like us, were traveling evangelists. We were very impressed with the travel trailer—it was exactly what we were looking for.

We had been invited to spend all the time necessary to examine it. While measuring the miniature closets to see if our stuff would fit, we opened a large drawer under one of the twin beds. To our utter amazement and disappointment, we found a pile of pornography. As you might imagine, in a flash this couple's "spiritual stock" (in our eyes) plummeted. Hell certainly smiled to see the minister's porn-filled drawer.

What people seldom realize—as I'm sure this minister and his wife didn't—is that such evil possessions invite the devil in, giving him permission to make himself at home. When demonic spirits make themselves at home, they set out to harass, to influence and to manipulate family members to more illicit behavior. The spiritual atmosphere of the home gradually shifts as the cycle continues unabated. The Holy Spirit, grieved, withdraws as He did from Samson's life (see Judg. 16:20). And, as Christians, although we are in Christ, we are no longer in the place of God's blessing. Even worse—we are now spiritually vulnerable and have become an embarrassment to the Lord Jesus.

No doubt God's angels wring their hands, and God, wanting to bless and to protect us, sadly watches as we waste our opportunities. In our ignorance and in some cases our willful disobedience, we have forfeited the Father's blessings and His angelic assistance. The enemy has a field day.

The Predominant Spiritual Presence

The spirit world is real—it exists alongside the natural world. Sharing your home with you and your family may be both angelic and demonic spirits. Jesus said of the Holy Spirit that He was like a wind that can come and go on the earth (see John 3:8);

Coexisting with what we physically see are spirit beings belonging to two opposing kingdoms—Satan's kingdom of darkness and God's kingdom of light.

Satan is described as a roaring lion walking about the earth (see 1 Pet. 5:8). The ratio between the two, which is in constant flux, is one ingredient that establishes the spiritual atmosphere of your home. While it's true that most of us cannot see that dimension, nonetheless it is there. Coexisting with what we physically see are spirit beings belonging to two opposing kingdoms—Satan's kingdom of darkness and God's kingdom of light.

> We do not look at the things which are seen, but at the things which are not seen. For the things which are seen are temporary, but the things which are not seen are eternal (2 Cor. 4:18).

Babies and small children naturally see the spiritual dimension. They see angels and demons. In fact, when a child reports that there is a monster in his or her room and the parents shine a flashlight in the closet and under the bed to prove the child is mistaken, it's the parent, not the child, who needs instruction. Let us relate a story from our family life that convinced us that young people see into the spirit realm.

Once when our youngest son, Bryan, was about 14 years old, he came into the kitchen one morning for breakfast. He said, "Dad, the strangest thing happened to me last night as I was about to fall asleep. I looked up into the darkness of my room and against the ceiling I saw hundreds of demonic faces sneering, snarling and scowling at me."

"What did you do, Son?" I asked.

"I just told God how tired I was and asked Him if He would get rid of them."

"What did God say?" I pressed him.

"He said, 'No,' Dad."

"Did He tell you why?"

"Yes, sir. He said, 'Bryan, I want you to let them watch you sleep.'"

Wow! Can you imagine the humiliation experienced by a team of demons whose only job was to scare a young servant of the Lord as they watched him peacefully fall asleep amid their threats?

I said, "Bryan, go and get your Bible." When he returned
with his Bible I said, "Read Psalm 3 to me." He read:

> LORD, how they have increased who trouble me! Many are
> they who rise up against me. Many are they who say of me,
> "There is no help for him in God." But *You, O LORD, are a
> shield for me*, my glory and the One who lifts up my head. I
> cried to the LORD with my voice, and He heard me from
> His holy hill. *I lay down and slept; I awoke, for the LORD sus-
> tained me. I will not be afraid of ten thousands of people who have
> set themselves against me all around.* Arise, O LORD; save me,
> O my God! For You have struck all my enemies on the
> cheekbone; You have broken the teeth of the ungodly.
> Salvation belongs to the LORD. Your blessing is upon
> Your people (emphasis added).

"Bryan," I explained, "The Lord just let you experience
Psalm 3!"

GIFT OF DISCERNING SPIRITS

There is also a spiritual gift mentioned by the apostle Paul called
"discerning of spirits" (1 Cor. 12:10). This gift, which is demon-
strated in various ways on many levels, is the capacity to see or to
sense the spirit level in some form or other.

One expression of this gift is the ability to actually see spiritual beings. This shouldn't come as any surprise. After all, seeing
angels was commonplace in Scripture. A classic example involves
the prophet Elisha and his servant, who awoke only to discover
they were surrounded by an army on horses and chariots. The
servant became anxious. He was fearful for his life. Elisha told
him, "Don't be afraid. . . . There are more troops on our side than
on theirs." (2 Kings 6:16, CEV).

Then Elisha prayed saying, "LORD, I pray, open [my servant's] eyes that he may see" (2 Kings 6:17). And the Lord opened the young man's spiritual eyes and, to his complete surprise, he saw the whole mountain covered with an angelic host on horses and fiery chariots, ready to defend them!

GOOD AND EVIL SPIRITS

Many of you might be asking, Who are the angelic host? And who are the demons that they wage war against?

Angels are God's spiritual helpers. Angels have been used by God to minister on the earth almost from the beginning. Amazingly, there are 99 references to angels in the New Testament alone! Examples include:

Two angels appeared in Sodom (see Gen. 19).
God's angels met Jacob (see Gen. 32).
Angels appeared to Moses (see Exod. 3).
David interacted with an angel (see 1 Chron. 21:16).
An angel appeared to Mary to announce the birth of Jesus (see Luke 1).
An angel appeared in a dream to Joseph (see Matt. 1).
An angel ministered to Peter (see Acts 12).

The evil counterparts to God's helpers are demons, subject to Satan. Many believe that these dark spirits are the fallen angels of whom the Bible speaks—those angels that rebelled with Lucifer and were expelled from heaven with him and who were ultimately cast onto the earth (see Isa. 14:12-15; Luke 10:18). However, there are other plausible speculations as to what demons might actually be.

What we do know is that demons, like Satan, wander the earth. Some spirits aimlessly wander through buildings; others may be specifically assigned to them. Some portray themselves as ghosts or spirits of the departed dead. Why do they do this? They do this because they desperately seek to interact with humanity. Satan continues to seek whom he may devour (see Luke 11:24; 1 Pet. 5:8).

From our experience we also know that demonic spirits seem to crave a material presence. Therefore, they continually search for a physical object, be it a human or animal body, or an object made of wood or stone, which they can manipulate for their purposes.

SPIRITUAL HOUSEGUESTS

Why would we assume the ministry of angels would be less in our day than in the biblical accounts? According to the end-time prophecies of Jesus and references in the book of Revelation, angels are very active in the last days—and of course in heaven for eternity!

PRAYER ASSIGNMENT

Lord, You are my deliverer and King. Thank You for the Word of God that says in 1 John. 4:4, "You are of God, little children, and have overcome them, because He who is in you is greater than he who is in the world." With this authority that comes from Your living in me, Lord Jesus, I ask that You replace any demonic influence in my home right now with Your abiding peace. Reveal to me anything about my attitudes or behaviors that would be attractive to the enemy.
[List each issue the Lord brings to mind.]

Now Lord, please show me anything among my belongings that dishonors You, whether in my home, car or business. [List each belonging]. *I will destroy it in order to please You in every area of my life. Thank You for showing me the way. In Jesus' name I pray. Amen.*

Note

1. Sinichi Suzuki, quoted in Valerie Bell, *Getting Out of Your Kids' Faces and Into Their Hearts* (Grand Rapids, MI: Zondervan Publishing, 1994), pp. 76-77.

CHAPTER THREE

SYMPTOMS OF SPIRITUAL POLLUTION

We stood on the spot where a church had once stood. It was an eerie feeling to realize that the shattered building was now floating down the San Jacinto River, having been washed away by raging floodwaters.

The pastor told us of the problems his congregation had encountered with the building, including the escrow account, the unexplainable putrid odors and the odd behavior of certain people within the church.

"What could be causing all of this?" the pastor asked.

"It sounds to us like your land is defiled," I (Alice) answered.

"It's strange that you would say that. Did you know that the movie *Grave Secrets*, starring Patty Duke, was made about this neighborhood? The developers never told the residents who bought these homes that this was once a Native American burial ground. After the residents moved in, many of them began to smell strange odors, to have their light bulbs burst for no apparent reason and to experience increased sickness. Sadly, some of the residents filed lawsuits against the developers. Others simply left. Their homes stand abandoned today. I had hoped that we were located far enough away from the site of the actual burial ground to not be affected by it."

THE SYMPTOMS

The Old Testament speaks of defiled land more than 15 times. The Hebrew word translated "defiled" is *taw-may*, which means foul or contaminated, especially in a ceremonial or moral sense. Homes as well as land can be defiled or spiritually polluted.

In Numbers 25:1-13, we find the story of how the Israelites began to commit whoredom by sacrificing and bowing down to Baal of Peor, the god of Moab. The defilement had so permeated the entire tribe that one of the Israelite men brought a Midianite prostitute into the tabernacle where Moses and the congregation were worshiping.

When Phinehas the priest, also the grandson of Aaron the high priest, saw this, he stood, took a javelin in his hand and killed both the Israelite and the prostitute. As famed radio commentator Paul Harvey would say, "And now . . . the rest of the story." After the abomination was brought to this abrupt halt, the plague against the Israelites was stopped; but those who died in the plague numbered 24,000 (see Num. 25:8-9).

Do you see it? Their ongoing illnesses and the deaths of 24,000 people were the result of spiritual pollution! What a tragedy! But if we don't want illness invading our homes, we must be on the lookout for possible sources of defilement.

The first step in recognizing sources of defilement is to know the symptoms:

- Sudden chronic illness
- Recurrent bad dreams and nightmares
- Insomnia or unusual sleepiness
- Behavioral problems
- Relational problems—continual fighting, arguing and misinterpreted communication
- Lack of peace
- Restless, disturbed children
- Unexplained illness or bondage to sin
- Ghosts or demonic apparitions (to which young children are particularly susceptible)
- Poltergeists (the movement of physical objects by demons)
- Foul, unexplainable odors
- Atmospheric heaviness, making it hard to breathe
- Continual nausea and headaches

As cleansing the atmosphere for the Israelites stopped their problem, so also cleansing the atmosphere of our homes often solves these problems.

WHAT CONSTITUTES DEFILEMENT?

In the past, we have had the privilege of helping Christians throw out literally thousands of dollars worth of personal possessions that God revealed were defiling them and their homes. These were things that did not reflect the goodness, righteousness, truth and character of God. We have thrown out furniture, clothing, jewelry, paintings, occult items, sculptures, statues, books, magazines, records, posters, audiocassettes and videocassettes, religious icons and even rosary beads. What could possibly be wrong with rosary beads? Well, just as with any man-made item that assists people with prayer, the rosary—or similar items traditionally thought of as aids to prayer—can be used in idolatrous worship.

Ralph Woodrow, in his book *Babylon Mystery Religion,* writes,

> *The Catholic Encyclopedia* says, "In almost all countries, then, we meet with something in the nature of prayer-counters or rosary-beads." It goes on to cite a number of examples, including a sculpture of ancient Nineveh, mentioned by Layard, of two winged females praying before a sacred tree, each holding a rosary. For centuries, among the Mohammedans (Muslims), a bead-string consisting of 33, 66, or 99 beads has been used for counting the names of Allah. Marco Polo, in the thirteenth century, was surprised to find the King of Malabar using a rosary of precious stones to count his prayers. St. Francis Xavier and his companions were equally astonished to see that rosaries were universally familiar to the Buddhists of Japan. Among the Phoenicians a circle of beads resembling a rosary was used in the worship of Astarte, the mother goddess, about 800 B.C.[1]

If you are from a Catholic background, prayerfully consider the following events:

We were ministering in the northeast European nation of Latvia. Many people attended the meetings. However, the spiritual anointing on our lives seemed hindered for some unexplainable reason.

One night, as I (Eddie) was struggling to fall asleep, I cried out to the Lord, "Why, Lord? Why is it so difficult here?" I heard no answer. Soon I was fast asleep.

At approximately 3:00 A.M. I awoke suddenly from a deep sleep. I felt compelled to find a pen and paper. It was clear that the Father wanted to speak with me. For the next 20 minutes I wrote down what I seemed to hear Him say: "The spiritual restriction you are experiencing is a result of religious icons—specifically the crucifix."

I knew a crucifix was the symbol of Jesus on the cross. But why would the crucifix be a problem? I felt the Holy Spirit say, "The crucifix is a 'photograph' of Satan's finest hour. Whether carved in wood, chiseled in stone, painted in oils or molded in bronze, the crucifix presents to the world a dead, helpless God, which provokes many to pity and few to faith."

Then I remembered all of the nations we had visited. How many times we had seen images and icons of Jesus; 99 percent of them presented Him as weak, emaciated, sickly or dead. What of his mother, Mary? She was represented as vivacious, attractive and full of health. Often you would find her holding His emaciated body—although Scripture never suggests that she did. The Cross was not a tragedy, it was a victory!

The Holy Spirit continued, "The Crucifixion is not the point of the gospel. The open tomb is the point of the gospel. Go back and read the sermons in the New Testament." I did. Sure enough, the apostles preached, "With wicked hands you crucified Jesus, *but God has raised* Him up and He has ascended on high!" (We urge you to stop now and read Acts 2:23-36; 3:15; 4:10; 5:30-31; 10:39-41; 13:28-37; 17:30-32.) It is true! The gospel message that the apostles preached contains three times as much about the Resurrection as the Crucifixion! Not only is the cross empty—THE TOMB IS EMPTY! He is a living Christ, not a dead Christ! The central issue of the gospel is not the cross but the tomb.

I was then reminded by the Holy Spirit of our visit to Jordan. In the plane was a photo of the king of Jordan. On the airport wall in Amman, Jordan, was a bigger-than-life photo of the king of Jordan. His picture was in our cab. As we drove through the streets, we saw his picture on billboards and painted on buildings. It was in our hotel lobby. The Lord reminded me that by keeping an image before the people, you reinforce the message.

Then God brought to mind what Paul wrote in 1 Corinthians 15:13-14:

> But if there is no resurrection of the dead, then is Christ not risen. And if Christ is not risen, then our preaching is empty and your faith is also empty.

My heart broke to realize that nations that have elevated and embraced the crucifix, with its dead, helpless Jesus, have been the hardest to reach with the gospel of Christ.

The following night, we returned to the conference venue. We shared with the people the message we had received from the Lord. They were struck with the revelation. Joyfully and expectantly, they began to remove their necklaces and bracelets containing the crucifix. As they did, all heaven broke loose. People were born again and delivered. One of the most striking was the salvation and deliverance of a white witch.

We have learned through the years that it is one thing *to give things to God* in order that we might live for Him. But it is another thing altogether, as the rich young ruler learned, *to give up things for God* in order that we might die to this world and escape its hold on us.

When considering your possessions, don't forget religious paraphernalia! Perhaps your undue attachment to religious images is actually hindering instead of assisting your Christian walk. If you are struggling with this issue, just remember:

> However, when He, the Spirit of truth, has come, He will guide you into all truth; for He will not speak on His own authority, but whatever He hears He will speak; and He will tell you things to come (John 16:13).

LOVING HOUSECLEANING

Remember, spiritual housecleaning is not to be done out of fear or superstition; it is to be done out of wise and loving devotion to God. Our children need to see their parents as fearless examples to follow. They need to see the sufficiency of Christ in us. Our goal should be to have homes that honor Christ; homes in which He is comfortable and in which the presence of His Holy Spirit is predominant.

Although Christ soundly defeated Satan by His death on the cross, God has left the enemy here so that we might learn to overcome.

We have not been called to live life in a vacuum. We were born on a battlefield. Although Christ soundly defeated Satan by His death on the cross (see Col. 2:15), God has left the enemy here so that we might learn to overcome. God has promised to set His table before us "in the presence of [our] enemies" (Ps.

23:5). So fear not, brothers and sisters—Christ is our fortress and our shield and He will honor our efforts to keep a godly house. As we walk in obedience to Him, He assigns His angels to minister to us! Hebrews 1:14 says, "Are they not all ministering spirits sent forth to minister for those who will inherit salvation?"

PRAYER ASSIGNMENT

Father, Your Word is a light unto my path. Light my path right now, as You reveal any spiritual pollution from my family or from previous residents that is operating in my home. I repent for my ignorance and that of my forefathers (see Neh. 1:4-11). Wash me from these offenses with Your blood, Lord Jesus, and grant me complete freedom and victory. In Jesus' name I pray. Amen.

These are the items I am going to discard. (Make a list.)

These are the items I am going to sell. (Make a list.)

The money I receive from the sale of these items will go to_____.

Now, with your eyes open, say firmly:

In the powerful name of Jesus, I break any and all unholy contracts, agreements or alliances I have made with the kingdom of darkness and I command you, demons, to leave my home, my family and me—now!

Next, get up and find these items and place them in a trash bin or carefully burn them in a safe place. If an item is valuable and is not intrinsically evil—that is, it has unfavorable meaning only to you—sell it or give it away. Be free!

Note

1. Ralph Woodrow, *Babylon Mystery Religion* (Riverside, CA: Ralph Woodrow Evangelistic Association, Inc., 1966), p. 27, quoting *The Catholic Encyclopedia*, vol. 15, pp. 459 and 484.

CHAPTER FOUR

CAUSES OF SPIRITUAL POLLUTION

Before God called me (Alice) into the ministry, I was a real estate agent in northwest Houston. I had one listing that puzzled me—it was an attractive home in an upper-middle-class neighborhood and was newly painted inside and out, with updated wallpaper and carpeting. Potential buyers seemed to be impressed with the house and were constantly expressing an interest. Yet for some reason, it simply wouldn't sell.

The young Christian couple seeking to sell the home was equally confused and disappointed. After praying with them about the sale, we decided to have a team of intercessors pray through the property. As the prayer team drove up to the vacant house, our youngest son, Bryan, said, "Mother, I believe the Lord just showed me that there are satanic symbols painted on both the inside walls of the garage and on the ceiling of this house."

Since I had been through the house countless times and would have certainly noticed those things had they been there, I politely thanked him and told him I didn't think that was the case! He must have been mistaken.

However, when we walked in, out of respect to my son, I mentioned to the owners what he had told me. They looked at each other in shock. The wife explained, "The last renters of this house spray painted satanic symbols on the walls of the garage. As you know, we have repainted, but come with me; and I'll show you a bit of the design that can still be seen behind the hot water heater." Sure enough, just as she said, we could still see the partial outline of a pentagram. But where were the symbols on the ceiling? The ceiling hadn't been repainted and there were no satanic symbols visible.

Then Eddie remarked, "Wait a minute. There are two ceilings in this house. The one we see, and the ceiling in the attic space that we cannot see." We found the stairway, climbed into the attic with our flashlight and to our amazement there was a large black pentagram spray-painted on the ceiling in the attic space.

We led the owners in repenting on behalf of the renters for having defiled their home. Then we went through the house, anointed it with oil and dedicated it to the Lord. As we drove away, we sensed in our hearts that God had heard us and that the curse had been lifted. Sure enough, after being on the market for more than six months, their home sold for full price fewer than 12 hours later!

A Demonic Visitation Versus a Demonic Habitation

If you engage in intercession and effective spiritual ministry, you possibly will encounter demonic spirits from time to time. Jesus certainly did when He walked the earth. Like Jesus, we will never have the luxury of living in a demon-free zone. To the contrary, we are in a real spiritual war and Satan is not shooting blanks. It is serious business to be serious about Christ and His kingdom! But there is a difference between *a demonic habitation* and *a demonic visitation*.

We are in a real spiritual war and Satan is not shooting blanks.

The house we mentioned earlier had become a habitation of demons. In such cases, demons are assigned to, or have simply decided to dwell in, certain locations. In this case demonic spirits had been attracted there by the sin of the previous renters.

Such a habitation is quite different from the visitation often encountered by those who serve God. In fact, if you plan to serve God on the front lines of Kingdom warfare, you are going to occasionally confront the enemy. They will *visit* you from time to time. Trust us, we know!

One night after a very intense deliverance of a young woman, we were awakened to what sounded like golf-ball-size hail beating on our roof. Yet we were totally shocked as we looked out the window. There wasn't any rain, hail or even the slightest breeze. But the demonic visitation was still present. We weren't going to let the enemy intimidate us—we commanded the angry demons to shut up and leave us alone. The noise stopped and we fell asleep.

When we obey the Holy Spirit, He is pleased to manifest His peaceful presence. When we obey evil spirits they are pleased to manifest their impure presence. This apparently has to do with legal ties or contract rights we give them.

Have you ever been intimidated by the devil? What did you do about it?

AIMLESS OR ASSIGNED?

A friend of ours who is a pastor explained a night visitation in which a demon began trying to strangle him in his sleep. We have experienced this before, so we could understand his alarm. We said, "Pastor, can't you just imagine the poor demon who drew the lot to take on the assignment of strangling you? We're sure he begged and pleaded not to go, but his boss sent him anyway." We're convinced that in many cases it's more painful for demons than it is for us!

However, *a demonic visitation* is not the same as *a demonic habitation*. When demons *inhabit* a place, just as when they inhabit a person, it will require the ministry of deliverance to evict them. In a real sense, deliverance for a dwelling is much like deliverance for a person. One identifies the offenses that were committed, destroys the contracts made with darkness, removes the things that seal and symbolize the contract and attract or enable darkness, and then dedicates one's home to God.

SOURCES OF DEFILEMENT

Sources of spiritual defilement can take any shape. Below is a list—some items are always instruments of the darkness; others can become such instruments due to our unhealthy attachment to them. (This list of offensive items is representative, not comprehensive.)

- Things related to heathen worship (voodoo dolls, spirit masks, snakes, dragons, thunderbirds, phoenixes, etc.)
- Things related to past sin (necklace, ring, love letters, photos)
- Things with unknown history, which are not inherently evil by design (Pray about the item. Dedicate it to the Lord. If the problem persists, then discard it.)
- Things that have become gods in our lives (collections, antiques, clothing, money, jewelry, etc.)
- Ouija Board (also known as a witch's board)
- Games like *Dungeons and Dragons, Masters of the Universe, Pokemon* (a combination of the words "pocket" and "monster") and certain video games with witchcraft references, extreme violence, demonic or occult entities and images
- Buddhist, Hindu or other Eastern worship artifacts
- Certain indigenous art or pagan worship items, Egyptian ankh (the cross with a loop on top)
- Items related to satanism, witchcraft, New Age, yoga, Unity, zodiac, crescent moon, crystal ball, pyramids (ancient obelisks or the Asherah poles of the Old Testament) and the martial arts
- Things related to astrology, horoscopes and geomancy, Edgar Cayce, Jean Dixon
- Comic books, rock posters, hard rock music and materials with obvious images of darkness
- Pornographic materials of any kind (including explicit sexual videos, books, cable and satellite TV channels and Internet sites)
- Art with obvious demonic representations such as snakes, spirits, death, gargoyles, skulls, dragons, etc.
- Material related to Mormonism, Jehovah's Witness, Unity Church, Scientology, ancestral worship, Islam, Rosicrucianism, Zen, Hare Krishna, etc.

- Things relating to secret societies like Freemasonry, Eastern Star, Knights of Malta, Skull and Bones, etc.
- Certain children's books or movies, such as *Harry Potter,* which encourage children to seek access to spiritual power unauthorized by God
- Good luck charms, amulets, fetishes
- Masonic aprons, books or rings, oriental yin and yang symbols, fortune-telling with tea leaves, tarot cards, talisman, etc.
- Movies with occult messages, extreme violence, excessive foul language or explicit sexual content
- Books (novels that focus on sensuality or death and destruction)

Perhaps you are thinking that some of the above-mentioned items are harmless—and even fun. But dealings with the devil are never harmless. We always pay a price.

Never has that been clearer to us than during a revival meeting we were conducting in a southern Texas church some years ago. A lady and her daughter walked down the aisle and tearfully shared with us how they had consulted a Ouija board the night before:

> We sat on either side of the board and followed the instructions. We asked, "What is your name?" The pointer, haltingly at first, then very directly, spelled "Death." Then we asked it, "Where are you from?" The pointer spelled "Satan." Fear filled our hearts. We asked finally, "How far does your power reach?" The board then spelled, "To the blood."

In case you have further doubts regarding the innocence of something like a Ouija board, listen to God's warning in

Deuteronomy 18:9-14:

> When thou art come into the land which the LORD thy
> God giveth thee, thou shalt not learn to do after the
> abominations of those nations. There shall not be found
> among you any one that maketh his son or his daughter
> to pass through the fire, or that useth divination, or an
> observer of times, or an enchanter, or a witch, or a
> charmer, or a consulter with familiar spirits, or a wizard,
> or a necromancer. *For all that do these things are an abomi-*
> *nation unto the* LORD *and because of these abominations* the
> LORD thy God doth drive them out from before thee.
> Thou shalt be perfect with the LORD thy God. For these
> nations, which thou shalt possess, hearkened unto
> observers of times, and unto diviners: but as for thee, the
> LORD thy God hath not suffered thee so to do (*KJV,*
> emphasis added).

HEATHEN SOUVENIRS

A retired missionary couple sought our help with their rebellious, drug-addicted teenage son. We were appalled upon visit-
ing their home to find their entire house decorated with heathen
worship artifacts they had brought back as souvenirs from the
foreign mission field where they had served. They thought their
home was a display of cultural curios, when in fact their souvenirs were nothing less than images of demonic gods! They
never guessed that their home was a satanic shrine! Can you
image how that grieved the Holy Spirit? Is God bringing to mind
anything like this in your home?

One instance that comes to my mind involved a family that
I (Alice) led to Christ. A ghost continually troubled their two

preschool sons. Our investigation revealed a large painting in their living room. This beautiful Southwest Indian painting seemed harmless at first. The painting depicted the body of a fallen Indian brave being burned on his funeral pyre. Above the flames the brave's "spirit man" rode his "spirit horse" and ascended into paradise.

The label on the back of the painting explained that the artist was a shaman, who came from a long lineage of shamans. It further explained that this particular artist assigned a spirit being to each of the paintings he produced. Sure enough, when the painting was removed (without the knowledge of the small boys), the ghost (demonic spirit) was never seen again.[1]

God is very clear when He reveals the things in our lives that will bring blessings or curses. For example, He states, "Cursed be the man that maketh any graven or molten image, an abomination unto the LORD, the work of the hands of the craftsman, and putteth it in a secret place" (Deut. 27:15, KJV).

EVEN STEPHEN KING?

One family who had a problem with spiritual entities roaming through their house at night invited us to pray through their home. The Lord revealed several unholy things throughout the

---

Satan is clever; he'll use any available means to separate you from God's will for your life.

---

evening as we prayed through each room. We were about to leave when we asked, "What's in the attic?"

"Nothing," the father replied. "We don't keep things in our attic."

"Yes, you do," we persisted. "The Lord just told us that one of your problems is in the attic. How do we get up there?"

The husband led us into the garage and placed a ladder under the opening. When we crawled into the attic we discovered a large cardboard box in a corner filled with Stephen King novels. The previous owners had left them there. That night we removed the books and the supernatural defilement ended.

You never know where you might find defilement. Keep an open mind—Satan is clever; he'll use any available means to separate you from God's will for your life.

HALLOWEEN

This chapter wouldn't be complete without touching on the issue of Halloween. Now keep in mind that 30 years ago, when we were new parents, each October 31 we would dress our kids in costumes and take them door-to-door in our neighborhood to trick-or-treat. We were sensitive enough to the Lord not to dress them as witches, skeletons, monsters or other evil personages. Since we did this for the enjoyment of our children, we didn't feel that we were participating in anything ungodly.

However, light (revelation) is given where light is received. In His time God began to reveal to us that Halloween is inherently evil. This is because although Halloween is a religious day, it is not a Christian day. The origin of Halloween is the Celtic festival of Samhain, lord of death and evil spirits. Long before Christ (over 2,000 years ago), Druids in Britain, Ireland, Scotland, France, Germany and other Celtic countries observed the end of summer by making sacrifices to Samhain. The Celts considered November 1 as being the day of death because the leaves were falling. They believed that Muck Olla, their sun god, was losing strength and Samhain, lord of death, was overpowering him. Further, they believed that on October 31, Samhain assembled the spirits of all who had died during the previous year.

Druid priests would lead the people in diabolical worship ceremonies in which horses, cats, black sheep, oxen, human beings and other offerings were rounded up, stuffed into wicker cages and burned to death. This was done to appease Samhain and keep spirits from harming them, for it was believed at this time that all of the wandering spirits would get hungry. If you set out a treat for them, they would not trick or curse you. Hence we have the origin of trick or treat. Tom Sanuinet, former high priest of Wicca, had this to say about Halloween:

> Trick or treat is a reenactment of the Druidic practices. The candy has replaced the human sacrifices of old, but it is still an appeasement of those deceptive evil spirits. The traditional response to those who do not treat is to have a trick played on them. Giving Halloween candy is symbolic of a sacrifice to false gods. You are participating in idolatry.[2]

When we began to see the spiritual implications associated with celebrating Halloween, we decided that it was not pleasing to the Lord Jesus. So instead of celebrating Halloween, we decided to celebrate our children every October 31. We would turn off our porch light (a signal to others that we were not participating in the festivities), take our children to their favorite restaurant and then to their favorite entertainment. We ended the evening by taking them to the candy aisle of the local grocery. They were allowed to fill a bag with the candy of their choice. They were thrilled! As parents, we weren't preventing them from enjoying Halloween; we were celebrating them! And there was no need to worry about razor blades or needles in their candy.

In recent years, local churches have begun offering Halloween alternatives, harvest festivals, prayer vigils and glory gatherings where all references to Halloween are removed and instead wholesome games are played, Christian songs are sung and Christian videos shown. Others are using Halloween as a night to pass out gospel literature. Whatever you choose to do, "Do not be overcome by evil, but overcome evil with good" (Rom. 12:21).

ONE MORE NIGHT WITH THE FROGS

Now that we've examined where those cobwebs might be found in your spiritual house, let's talk about just how clean you want your house to be. Most people want their homes to be spotless; isn't that what we should want for our souls as well?

Most people want their homes to be spotless; isn't that what we should want for our souls as well?

Not everyone wants to be so thoroughly cleansed. When we meet such folk, we are reminded of Moses and Pharaoh. We've always been intrigued by Pharaoh's answer to Moses regarding the plague of frogs in Egypt. You'll remember that God sent a plague of frogs and the Egyptian magicians added to it. Interestingly, in their attempt to "compete" with God, they only compounded Pharaoh's problem! The Egyptians had frogs in their bread and frogs in their beds—they had been overrun by frogs!

Then Pharaoh called for Moses and Aaron, and said, "Entreat the LORD that He may take away the frogs from me and from my people; and I will let the people go, that they may sacrifice to the LORD. And Moses said to Pharoah, *"Accept the honor of saying when I shall intercede for you, for your servants, and for your people, to destroy the frogs from you and your houses, that they may remain in the river only."* So [the Pharoah] said, *"Tomorrow."* And [Moses replied], "Let it be according to your word, that you may know that there is no one like the LORD our God" (Exod. 8:8-10, emphasis added).

Pharaoh's palace was littered with frogs; yet when Moses asked him, "When do you want me to rid you of these frogs?" Pharaoh replied, "Tomorrow." *Tomorrow!?* What's wrong with *right now*?! Why would anyone want to live one more night with the frogs!?

Are you content with one more night with the frogs? Some Christians are willing to live lives that are *almost* plague free. Free enough to get to church once a week. Free enough to live a moral life. But not free enough to really impact the kingdom of darkness by extending the kingdom of God.

LIVING IN THE SPIRIT

At this point you might be wondering what steps you can take to avoid encountering such defilement in your life. The answers are all in God's Word. Read it; study it. Keep God's most important commands close to your heart. We have been commanded to walk in the light if we are to have fellowship with Christ (see 1 John 1:7).

And have no fellowship with the unfruitful works of darkness (Eph. 5:11).

But you are a chosen generation, a royal priesthood, a holy nation, His own special people, that you may proclaim the praises of Him who called you out of darkness into His marvelous light (1 Pet. 2:9).

The night is far spent, the day is at hand. Therefore let us cast off the works of darkness, and let us put on the armor of light (Rom. 13:12).

Do not quench the Spirit. Abstain from every form of evil (1 Thess. 5:19,22).

Do not give the devil a foothold (Eph. 4:27, *NIV*).

PRAYER ASSIGNMENT

Lord Jesus, I am so sorry for my involvement in the occult, which I thought was harmless. Now I realize it was not harmless. I see it and I repent in Your presence. Please cleanse me from my sin and free me from the devil's torment.

Make a list of books, artwork and items that God is speaking to you about removing.

(With eyes open) I command any spirit of witchcraft or antichrist spirit to leave me now. You have no right to my life. In the powerful name of Jesus, I command you to leave my home, my family, my possessions and me!

Notes

1. Art from most cultures is based on religious or spiritual images and influences. A classic example is the use of the dragon in Chinese art. The dragon is one of the Bible's descriptions of Satan. Western art, for the most part, is based on natural images and influences (i.e., seascapes, landscapes, portraits). When it comes to artwork, we should exercise caution and discernment.

    Much Native-American art has no spiritual implications whatsoever. I (Eddie) am part Cherokee, so I am not criticizing any people group.

2. Christian Youth Alliance, Long Beach Island Student Center, Ship Bottom, New Jersey, e-mail: cya@computer.net.

WHERE YOU NEVER THOUGHT TO LOOK

Years ago, a woman who had suffered bondage and sickness for many years asked us to send a team to pray through her house. As Eddie walked past her desk the Lord gave him an impression.

"I believe this lower drawer is filled with some sort of defilement," he said. She opened the drawer and pulled out a shoe box filled with love letters. As tears welled up in her eyes and her voice cracked with emotion, she explained that the letters were from an inmate in the state penitentiary. She had once been his pen pal.

The prisoner had written passionate letters about his deep feelings for her. Later, however, she learned that it was all a lie.

He was deceitfully cultivating a phony relationship with her so that he could list her among his references in order to procure an early release from incarceration. Sadly, he had even proposed marriage to the lonely woman, although he never had true romantic intentions.

"Why do you keep these letters that are filled with lies?" we asked.

She tearfully admitted, "Sometimes on lonely nights I pull out this box, curl up by the fire and read them, trying to refeel my faded dreams."

We explained that she had allowed a stronghold of lies to be built in her mind. The letters were symbolic of the enemy's successful campaign. Finally, she began to get angry at the deception she had embraced and agreed to renounce the contracts she had made with lying spirits.

It's time for the Church to get angry over what Satan has done! Many Christians feel anger is sin. Not necessarily! Scripture says, "Be ye angry, and sin not" (Eph. 4:26, *KJV*). Paul urges us to "abhor that which is evil" (Rom 12:9, *KJV*). This woman's healing and freedom came as she burned the letters.

UNHOLY SOUL TIES

While ministering to a woman who had been diagnosed as having 127 personalities (see "multiple personality disorder" in the glossary), we noticed that she wore a strange pendant. We asked who had given it to her. She mentioned her best friend, explaining that they had exchanged pendants with each other.

"Your friend has the same diagnosis as you, doesn't she?" we inquired.

She nodded yes. Sure enough, her friend was hospitalized with multiple personality disorder as well. Both of them were demonized and bound together in an unholy alliance (see glossary). The necklaces were symbols of their union. She could not be set free until the necklace was destroyed and she renounced the unholy soul tie.

After our team of ladies ministered to her for three days she went home free—with only one joyful, Christ-filled personality!

> Is it possible that our failure to purify our homes and our lives is keeping God's Word from prevailing mightily? We believe so.

We have worked with several people who have suffered from depression and related symptoms. Amazingly, many of them came to freedom when they destroyed their spiritual journals or diaries in which they had unwittingly recorded their negative, depressing thoughts. They had documented the enemy's success by writing down their "stinking thinking." They had given the devil a foothold by logging their complaints against God, declaring—even documenting—the devil's effectiveness in their lives!

The above is an example of what we call an unholy soul tie. Such ties can include souvenirs, trinkets, books, stuffed animals, photos, music albums, jewelry, love letters, clothing, furniture and wall hangings.

Many Christians have things in their possession that relate to their past sins. When we possess things that are associated with the sinful relationships of our former lives without Christ, we insult God. It also delights the enemy and strengthens his hold on our lives. Remove old love letters; rid yourself of jewelry and clothing that represent and encourage emotional, physical, psychological or spiritual attachment; break free from old things and walk in the newness of God!

> Many who had believed came confessing and telling their deeds. Also, many of those who had practiced magic brought their books together and burned them in the sight of all. And they counted up the value of them, and it totaled fifty thousand pieces of silver [a piece of silver was about a day's wage]. *So the word of the Lord grew mightily and prevailed* (Acts 19:18-20, emphasis added).

Is it possible that our failure as Christ's Church to purify our homes and our lives is keeping God's Word from prevailing mightily? We believe so.

In a revival meeting in Oklahoma, we had the opportunity to lead a young pastor's wife to salvation and deliverance. For some time she had been involved in an extramarital affair with a teenage boy who was also a member of their church. We led her to Christ and then walked her through repentance, reconciliation and deliverance concerning the matter. But within a few weeks she again was being severely tempted and harassed by demonic spirits.

One night she called us long distance to explain her problem. We asked if she still had any gifts that the boy had given her. She remembered a necklace and a blouse. We suggested that she destroy them completely. They were symbols of the sinful contract she had made with the enemy. She and her husband burned the blouse and shattered the necklace, and the attachment was broken, freeing her from her past.

Throughout history, when men have made covenants and contracts with each other, they have sealed them with the giving of gifts (see 1 Sam. 18:3-4). Therefore, it is important not only to break the contracts but also to rid ourselves of the gifts that symbolize and seal the contracts that we've made. Do you have any souvenirs of sin? Have you cleaned your closets lately?

> And what agreement hath the temple of God with idols? For *ye are the temple of the living God*; as God hath said, I will dwell in them, and walk in them; and I will be their God, and they shall be my people. *Wherefore come out from among them, and be ye separate, saith the Lord, and touch not the unclean thing; and I will receive you,* And will be a Father unto you, and ye shall be my sons and daughters, saith the Lord Almighty. Having therefore these promises, dearly beloved, let us cleanse ourselves from all filthiness of the flesh and spirit, perfecting holiness in the fear of God (2 Cor. 6:16–7:1, *KJV*, emphasis added).

POSSESSIONS WITH AN UNKNOWN PAST

Sometimes items in our homes have an unknown past. They may be things that we've inherited, found by chance or purchased.

When we were newly wed, we lived on a modest income. We used to tease that our home was decorated in early pawnshop. Actually, early garage sale would have been a bit closer to the truth!

Now let's be realistic—not superstitious. Let's say that you have an antique family heirloom about which you know little or nothing. Should you discard it? Read on.

After the Israelites' loss at Ai, we read how they soundly defeated Jericho. Joshua and his men were instructed by God to take the gold, silver, brass and iron vessels of Jericho back to be used in the service of the Lord (see Josh. 6:24). Later, after the successful battle against Ai, God gave Israel all the cattle and the spoils of the city (see Josh. 8:27). In Egypt, the children of Israel were told upon their departure to borrow jewels, silver, gold and clothing from the Egyptians for their journey (see Exod. 12:35-36). They weren't concerned about any defilement from these items because God had given them the okay.

If an item has an unknown history and is without obvious evil overtones, still exercise wise judgment. If you have a spiritual uneasiness about the item, pray and sanctify it unto the Lord. For that matter, all of your possessions should be given to God. Afterward, if there is still a question, put that particular item out of your house (perhaps in your garage) for a time. (It should go without saying, don't ask anyone else to keep it at his or her house!) Look for any evidence that it was causing problems. If there is evidence, get rid of it! If, after removing the object, the same restlessness is present in the home, then the problem lies in another area. So keep searching until you find the culprit. And remember, no material possession is worth more than the sweet, peaceful presence and protection of the Holy Spirit!

SINS OF THE PREVIOUS OWNERS

A young family from our church needed my (Eddie's) help. Neither of their two young sons had ever peacefully slept in the baby's room, which was located next to the master bedroom. When their second son was born, they moved their oldest son across the house to a third bedroom, where he soundly slept for the first time in three years. But what was the problem in the baby's room?

My son and I dropped in one night to pray. We went through the baby's room with a fine-tooth comb. There was no object that was representative of evil. From the wallpaper to the toys, it seemed the perfect room in which a baby could rest.

Then the Lord showed Bryan three evil spirits standing in the center of the room. "Son, describe them to me," I said. He did. One appeared as an old woman, another as an old man—but "One," he said, "is huge, Dad!"

"Well, let's start with the big one," I said dryly. At that, he burst out laughing.

"What's so funny?" I asked.

"Dad," he replied, "you should have seen the look on his face when he heard you say, 'Let's start with the big one.'"

We cleansed the nursery and blessed it. These three spirits had undoubtedly disturbed the babies' sleep. But I wondered what had given them a right to be in the home of this loving Christian family?

I found the answer when we turned to leave and something unusual caught my eye. There was a screen door eye screwed into the door jam, *outside* of the bedroom door. And there was a corresponding hole on the *outside* of the bedroom door where there had once been a screen door hook—it must have been placed there to keep a child in the room.

When we arrived home, I mentioned this to Alice. She told me, "Eddie, I sold the house to its current owner. They bought the house from a police officer. He and his wife had one preschool son. Honey, that man was one of the worst fathers I've ever seen. As we were signing the closing papers, he cursed and criticized the little boy the entire time."

It then became clear to me that the previous owners had locked their little boy in his room when they didn't want to be bothered. As speaker and author George Otis, Jr., often says, "In trauma the soul solicits many saviors." When that little boy was locked in the room, spirits of darkness befriended him. They can do that, you know. Demons "minister" to your needs until you think you can count on them. Once they've sucked you in, they seek to destroy you (see John 10:10).

The current owners reported that from that night forward there were no more problems with the children sleeping in that room.

The activities of the previous residents in your home could have lingering effects for you and your family. The real estate closing settles the issue of physical ownership. Spiritual ownership and authority, however, can be an entirely different matter.

One family discovered that from the moment they took ownership of their home, soon after the closing, they were in financial trouble. We asked, "Did you get the house at a good price?"

"Oh yes," the husband explained, "it was a foreclosure."

When they repented to God for the financial sins of the previous owners, breaking any curses on the property and consecrating it to the Lord, they experienced an immediate financial breakthrough.

The same is true of family violence, divorce and other relational sins committed by previous owners, activating and releasing forces that defile the property. The forces can be expelled and their contracts with former owners annulled.

Houses, graveyards, "sacred" groves or places deemed by New Agers or witches to have special powers or which have been dedicated to demons may at times require deliverance ministry. But they need not be destroyed. What do you think? Could your home have similar problems?

OTHER PEOPLE'S PROPERTY?

Suppose you have an unsaved roommate who has a collection of occult literature. Or perhaps you have an unsympathetic or lost family member who has possessions that dishonor God in the very house you share with him or her. What are you to do?

Clearly, you have no right to destroy or remove someone else's property. We suggest that you gather as many facts as possible beforehand and then appeal to them in love. Your presentation should be well thought-out and prepared. Don't base your request on superstition. The Church has too many superstitious Christians now. Base your request upon Scripture, your love for God, your respect for His holiness and your desire to live under His protection and blessing. Spend some time praying and listening to God for His words of wisdom and direction before you attempt to make your case. Then do so with love, gentleness and respect.

Should that fail, then appeal to God. Ask the Lord to intervene on your behalf and also to provide protection for you. Remember that Moses was reared in Pharaoh's home and Joseph served in Potiphar's house in Egypt—both residences would have been filled with heathen worship artifacts. Yet both of these men were protected and mightily used of God!

When it seems that we are left with no alternatives, we can still live with God's blessing in any environment. We can purify our lives and possessions. We can purify our living spaces and announce to the enemy whose children we are and clearly delineate what does and what does not belong to us!

PARENTAL RESPONSIBILITIES

Parent, what about your children's possessions? When dealing with preschool children simply remove the offensive items. However, for older children it could be a useful teaching opportunity to tell them the issues behind some of the toys, games and books that may be defiled. As parents, we must be sensitive and loving in any endeavor of this nature. We must not project mental images that provoke fear.

Of course, many of our children are sensitive to the Lord. They love God and really want to please Him. Show them how to pray over their own possessions and decide what honors Christ and what doesn't. Once they know the facts, many children take delight in ridding themselves of defilement.

Show your children how to pray over their own possessions and decide what honors Christ and what doesn't.

As parents, each of us must decide how we will parent our children. We suggest that you first appeal to your children in love. Should that prove ineffective, then exercise your right as a parent and property owner. As property owners, we will simply not allow certain things to enter our homes. Please listen to God, then decide together what you will and will not allow. You will, as we have, draw a line somewhere. Will you allow just any type of music to be played in your home? Will you allow rock posters to be taped to your walls? Will you allow tobacco or illegal drug use in your home? Will you allow pornography? Are you going to permit premarital sex in your home? What about a satanic altar?

We have seen parents, at times, wrestle with each of these things in regard to their children. You too will draw a line somewhere! But remember, if you give the devil a toehold in your home, it will soon become a stronghold! Give the enemy an inch and he'll take a mile!

EFFECTIVE DEFILEMENT PATROL

A father called us in a panic late one night. He said, "Folks, I've just got to have your help. Our 17-year-old son is upstairs in his room right now. He's got heavy metal, acid rock music blaring, demonic rock-and-roll posters stapled to his walls, and he's up there right now smoking marijuana. What should I do?"

"Have you asked him to remove these things from his room?" we asked.

"Yes, but he won't do so," the father sheepishly replied.

"What he needs more than anything is a daddy," we said.

"I'm his daddy," he replied.

"No, sir, you're his father." Eddie said. "A daddy establishes boundaries. Once your son violates the boundaries, go into the room, rip the posters off the wall, flush the marijuana down the toilet and remove the stereo! If that doesn't work, take his door off the hinges and store it in the garage. If he still doesn't get it, begin taking his furniture out a piece at a time. When he's left with a blanket and a pillow and is sleeping on the floor, he may get the point." A godly daddy will say, as Joshua did, "As for me and my house, we will serve the LORD" (Josh. 24:15).

Such drastic measures are rarely needed, thank God! But it may be helpful for your family to sit down together and decide what will be considered acceptable attitudes, behaviors and possessions in your home. You might even write a contract for both you and your children to sign.

Do you agree with the plan of action we have presented? If not, how has God instructed you to handle this important issue?

LEGALISM AND SUPERSTITION

If Satan can't convince us to keep things that defile our lives, he will provoke us to legalism and superstition. In either case, he wins.

I (Alice) received a call from a woman who was obsessed with fear. I took a prayer team of ladies with me to visit in her home. We were absolutely shocked when we saw that she had pinned prayer cloths to her curtains, her pictures, her bedspread and even to her body.

"Where have you pinned prayer cloths to your body?" I asked. She raised her blouse; draped from her bra were several two-inch-square pieces of white cloth attached by safety pins.

If Satan can't convince us to keep things that defile our lives, he will provoke us to legalism and superstition. In either case, he wins.

"Is this all?" I quizzed her.

"No," she tentatively replied. She pulled her slacks halfway down to reveal a dozen or more cloths pinned around her panty line.

"Why are you doing this?" I asked.

"I received these anointed prayer cloths from a television evangelist, and he promised they could protect me from evil."

This lady had fallen to superstition. Our righteous living and the goodness of God is our protection—not a useless, worn-out piece of cloth.

Remember, we should be neither legalistic and judgmental nor fearful and superstitious. We should be discerning and, above all, seek God's will and direction in these matters. Don't rush to judgment!

Should we refuse to subscribe to the newspaper because it contains an astrological column or beer ad? Be sensible; be careful and, above all, be obedient. After all, "to obey is better than sacrifice" (1 Sam. 15:22). Pray and seek godly counsel if necessary. God tells us to "let the peace of God rule in your hearts" (Col. 3:15).

PRAYER ASSIGNMENT

Father God, I love You and would never want to dishonor You. I am excited about all You are teaching me right now. Your revelation is setting me free. Reveal to me any areas of my past that need repentance. (Wait for the Lord now.)

I am sorry for the wrong relationships I have entered into. (Name each one.)

Cleanse me now and set me free from any hold the enemy has on me. Show me any object from a wrong relationship that I need to discard, and I will do it.

(Say aloud and with your eyes open) *Spirits of darkness, I break all unholy soul ties between me and* (make a list)

_____

_____

_____

I cancel all sexual perversion through fornication, adultery, pornography or mental lust in the name of Jesus. Heeding the words of Matthew 3:10, I lay an ax to any unfruitful root of darkness whether past or present.

Thank You, Father, for helping me. In Jesus' name I pray. Amen.

C H A P T E R   S I X

THE PURIFICATION PROCESS

In the Old Testament book of Leviticus, we read how the priests executed the rites of purification. Basically, they offered a sacrifice, performed an anointing with oil, announced the cleansing and pronounced a blessing. Once purified, they were able to enter into God's will for them—to be sanctified.

> Sanctify yourselves therefore, and be ye holy: for I am the LORD your God. And ye shall keep my statutes, and do them: I am the LORD which sanctify you. And ye shall be holy unto me: for I the LORD am holy (Lev. 20:7-8,26, *KJV*).

Reader, you are a priest and part of a kingdom of priests (see Rev. 1:6)! Consecrate yourself to the Lord, heeding the call of God through King Hezekiah to cleanse your life of defilement:

"Remove all defilement from the sanctuary. Our fathers were unfaithful; they did evil in the eyes of the LORD. Therefore, the anger of the LORD has fallen on Judah and Jerusalem; he has made them an object of dread and horror and scorn, as you can see with your own eyes. This is why our fathers have fallen by the sword and why our sons and daughters and our wives are in captivity." Then they went in to King Hezekiah and reported: "We have purified the entire temple of the LORD, the altar of burnt offering with all its utensils, and the table for setting out the consecrated bread, with all its articles. We have prepared and consecrated all the articles that King Ahaz removed in his unfaithfulness while he was king. They are now *in front of the LORD's altar*" (2 Chron. 29:5-6,8-9,18-19, *NIV*, emphasis added).

An important key to our victory is placing our lives and our possessions "before the LORD's altar."

PUT AWAY THE LEAVEN!

Leaven, in Scripture, represents sin, evil or false doctrine. For this reason the Lord called upon the Israelites to cleanse their homes of leaven, not just once but every year. Moses gave this instruction for the Israelites:

And this day shall be unto you for a memorial; and ye shall keep it a feast to the LORD throughout your generations; ye shall keep it a feast by an ordinance for ever.

Seven days shall ye eat unleavened bread; *even the first day ye shall put away leaven out of your houses*: for whosoever eateth leavened bread from the first day until the seventh day, that soul shall be cut off from Israel. And in the first day there shall be an holy convocation, and in the seventh day there shall be an holy convocation to you; no manner of work shall be done in them, save that which every man must eat, that only may be done of you. And ye shall observe the feast of unleavened bread; for in this selfsame day have I brought your armies out of the land of Egypt: therefore shall ye observe this day in your generations by an ordinance for ever. In the first month, on the fourteenth day of the month at even, ye shall eat unleavened bread, until the one and twentieth day of the month at even. *Seven days shall there be no leaven found in your houses:* for whosoever eateth that which is leavened, even that soul shall be cut off from the congregation of Israel, whether he be a stranger, or born in the land. Ye shall eat nothing leavened; in all your habitations shall ye eat unleavened bread (Exod. 12:14-20, *KJV*, emphasis added).

In the Jewish home the father would gather the family for this annual celebration. Before this observance, he would hide pieces of leavened bread in various places throughout the house to symbolize sin. Later during the celebration, the family members would search through the house for the hidden bits of leavened bread. The children especially enjoyed this traditional game.

As they found the bits of bread, the Jewish father would take a spoon, a dustpan and a feather and carefully sweep up each piece of leavened bread. After reading Scripture and praying together about hidden sin, the family would burn the leaven outside the house, symbolizing the removal of personal sin.

Remember, physical symbols often carry spiritual significance. For example, because Moses struck the rock twice, when God told him to strike it only once, he was not allowed to enter the Promised Land. Why? Well, it was more than simple disobedience; the rock represented Christ. Christ was stricken once for sin, not twice. Moses was denying God's symbol!

WHY DOES THE CHURCH LACK POWER?

By failing to obey God, as Moses did, we forfeit God's power in our lives. The Church's spiritual impotence should be a serious concern to us. Why do we lack power? Why is our authority over the enemy so compromised? Why does revival tarry?

Remember these lamentable words from Joshua 7:12-13 (emphasis added):

> Therefore *the children of Israel* could not stand before *their* enemies, but turned their backs before *their* enemies, because *they have become doomed to destruction*. Neither will I be with you anymore, unless you destroy the accursed from among you. Get up, sanctify the people, and say, "Sanctify yourselves for tomorrow, because thus says the LORD God of Israel, *'There is an accursed thing in your midst, O Israel; you cannot stand before your enemies until you take away the accursed thing from among you.'*"

Israel's armies had defeated Jericho, but now their own security had been compromised. They were powerless. They were fearful. Verse 5 says, "The hearts of the people melted and became like water." Amazingly, that's the very same description of Israel's enemies just a few days earlier. Now the tables had been turned.

What was the reason for their fear, intimidation and powerlessness against the enemies of God? Joshua wanted to know.

God gave him the answer: *"Israel has sinned,* and *they have also transgressed My covenant* which I commanded them. For they have even taken some of the accursed things . . . and they have also put it among their own stuff"* (Josh. 7:11, emphasis added). Remember? One man—Achan—had taken prohibited items from Jericho and hidden them among his own possessions in his house. Because of this, the whole nation was crippled!

The Church today is crippled because Christ's people are overlooking a necessary key that unlocks the door to revival: ridding our lives of those things that carry with them demonic defilement.

Just so, the Church today is crippled because Christ's people are overlooking a necessary key that unlocks the door to revival: ridding our lives of those things that carry with them demonic defilement. Are there accursed things in your home? Deuteronomy 7:25-26 warns us that objects of idolatry, even silver or gold, could ensnare us.

> You shall burn the carved images of their gods with fire; you shall not covet the silver or gold that is on them, nor take it for yourselves, lest you be snared by it; for it is an abomination to the LORD your God.
>
> Nor shall you bring an abomination into your house, lest you be doomed to destruction like it. You

shall utterly detest it and utterly abhor it, for it is an acursed thing (Deut. 7:25-26).

THE SEVEN STEPS OF PURIFICATION

Here are the steps God gave Joshua to take. Why don't you take them today?

1. Present yourself before the Lord for His inspection.

Self-evaluation is insufficient. Why? Because "the heart is deceitful above all things, and desperately wicked; Who can know it?" (Jer. 17:9).

We must do as David did. We must present ourselves to God for His inspection. David prayed, "Search me, O God, and know my heart; try me, and know my anxieties; and see if there is any wicked way in me, and lead me in the way everlasting" (Ps. 139:23-24).

If we really are honest with this process, we can ask our Christian family and godly friends for their insight to our lives as well.

2. Sanctify yourself. It is time that we sanctify ourselves and our possessions to the Lord.

To sanctify ourselves is to set ourselves apart for God alone. The word "sanctify" is from the Hebrew word *qadash,* which means "to set apart from a profane to a sacred purpose."[1] We need to commit to living sanctified lives before the Lord, putting off the old and receiving the new mandate to live in Christ.

As a deacon's wife began explaining to us about her daughter's involvement in satanism, the Lord gave us what some call a word of knowledge, or spiritual impression.

"Let's forget your daughter's satanism for a moment," we said. "Tell us about your husband's pornography." Sure enough, her husband was deeply involved in pornography. He had opened the door to the demonic. Now the demonic was destroying his daughter's life!

In another situation, a deacon loaned his adult son one of his blank videocassettes to record a favorite television program. Several days later, as the son watched his taped show end, child pornography suddenly appeared on the screen. The revealing tape was one that his father wished later he had not grabbed in such haste. Numbers 32:23 says, "Be sure your sin will find you out."

If you find yourself guilty of sin, bad attitudes or behavior, then repent (see 1 John 1:7-10). Not only are we to repent for our sins, but if we discover defilement on our property because of the sins of others, then we are to repent to God for that as well.

If you are aware of past wicked activities that have taken place on the property, you should repent on behalf of those who did them, just as Nehemiah repented on behalf of his countrymen and forefathers (see Neh. 1:6). This is called identificational repentance.

In her book *The Voice of God*, author and teacher Cindy Jacobs writes:

> What did Daniel do so God would release the people? He repented on their behalf, by admonishing, "We have sinned and committed iniquity" (see v. 5). This kind of praying was also done by Ezra and Nehemiah and is called "identificational repentance."
>
> Identificational repentance occurs when a person repents for the corporate sin of his or her nation. Does this mean that each person is not personally responsible before God for his or her own individual sins? Of course not. Each person must come to Christ for his or her own sins (see John 3:16; Rev. 20:13).[2]

3. Locate the offensive items.

Achan confessed that he had taken a beautiful Babylonian robe. Babylon, in Scripture, is said to be the seat of Satan or the center of evil in the earth. According to Ralph Woodrow, in his book *Babylon Mystery Religion*:

> Herodotus, the world traveler and historian of antiquity, witnessed the mystery religion and its rites in numerous countries and mentions how Babylon was the primeval source from which all systems of idolatry flowed. Bunsen says that the religious system of Egypt was derived from Asia and "the primitive empire in Babel."[3]

From the bounty of this pagan culture Achan had taken 200 shekels of silver and a wedge of gold weighing 50 shekels. "I coveted them," Achan said, "and took them" (Josh. 7:21). He loved those things more than he loved God. He desired their presence in his home more than he desired the Lord's presence. He admitted, "They are hidden in the ground inside my tent, with the silver underneath" (Josh. 7:21).

Are you willing to stand for holiness?

4. Rid yourself of those things that defile.

Remove anything that relates to the occult, to heathen worship and to sin. The only solution is to entirely remove them from the premises and destroy them completely, not give them away. These items attract demonic spirits and give them a right to inhabit your house; to fail to destroy these weapons of the enemy is to be an accomplice in his evil work (see Jas. 4:17).

That being said, remember, we do not have the right to destroy the property of others. However, we are responsible to act as God leads us, and as we fulfill His will, we are sanctified.

5. Be serious about this.

In the story of Joshua, once the Israelites obey the Lord and destroy their spoils, His favor rests upon them again. Immediately following their cleansing and repentance, Israel utterly destroyed the city of Ai along with its king! No enemy could stand before them!

You might be asking yourself, *This is the Old Testament. What does it have to do with me, today?* Paul explained, "Now *all these things happened unto them for examples*: and *they are written for our admonition*, upon whom the ends of the world are come. Wherefore let him that thinketh he standeth take heed lest he fall" (1 Cor. 10:11-12, *KJV*, emphasis added). If the demands of holiness were that great under the law, how much greater are they under grace?

6. Renounce the enemy and your association with him.

Break any contracts and unholy ties you have made with darkness, whether you made them willingly or unwillingly. Speak aloud: "I break any and all unholy soul ties that I made while in my ungodly relationship with _____ (name the person or sin). I sever these ties now by the blood of Jesus. In so doing, I take back any ground I gave the enemy in committing that sin." Please repeat this process for each item or, in some cases, each person.

7. Finally, consecrate your life and property to the glory of the Lord.

Some Christians choose to anoint their houses with oil. Oil is symbolic of the Holy Spirit. We call that a prophetic act. We can't say whether or not it is necessary. Each of us should seek the Lord's guidance in each situation.

Jesus created stories (called parables) to communicate His teaching points. In closing, we've created this parable for you.

THE PARABLE OF BILL AND MARY

Bill and Mary had been married for many years. Their kids were grown and no longer lived at home. Mary was a committed Christian, but Bill lived without Christ. His whole life revolved around his business.

One week Mary's church was having an evangelistic crusade. She convinced Bill to attend the Sunday-evening service with her. To make him more comfortable, they sat near the back of the auditorium. As the evangelist completed his message, he invited the audience to receive Christ. Bill suddenly began to experience something unfamiliar, as if God's finger was actually touching his heart. He felt exposed, unnerved, vulnerable—even lost. He listened to the story of Christ's death on Calvary and was overwhelmed by his own wickedness. He stumbled to the front of the auditorium and tearfully confessed his sin. He repented and invited Jesus Christ into his life and was wonderfully saved. Bill was a brand-new man! Mary and her friends were ecstatic! They had prayed for Bill's salvation for years.

That night Mary and Bill were almost asleep when Bill's heart abruptly became gripped by guilt. He tried to escape it, but he couldn't. He turned over and tearfully said, "Mary, I have something I need to confess to you."

"Are you referring to Janet?" Mary asked.

"Yes," Bill confirmed, "but how do you know about Janet and me?"

"Bill, I've known about your affair for two years," she replied.

Bill was amazed. "Could you ever find it in your heart to forgive me for sinning against you and God like I have?"

Mary smiled. Gently caressing his chin she said, "Sweetheart, tonight God forgave you of all your sins. I love you, and of course I forgive you." Bill fell fast asleep with a peace he had never before experienced.

The next day Bill left for work. He was born again! It was like starting his life afresh. He stopped on the way home from work to pick up flowers to take to Mary. He couldn't believe the warmth of their new Christ-centered relationship. *Why had he waited so long?* he asked himself.

Deal ruthlessly with Satan! Renounce his work. Remove his opportunities to hurt you, and start anew!

Tuesday morning he called home and invited Mary to meet him for lunch. The newness Christ had brought to their marriage was wonderful! Bill and Mary were experiencing genuine spiritual unity; and after all these years they finally were on the same page! That's why he was feeling newly wed.

Wednesday morning Bill was interrupted by his secretary's voice over the intercom. "Bill," she announced, "Janet is here to see you." It was as if Bill's blood had turned to iced water. *Oh, no! It's Janet!* he thought. Then it dawned on him that he had made everything right with God and with Mary, but he had forgotten to break his sinful relationship with Janet.

Do you get the point? It's important that you break off your former relationship with the enemy. He is unlawful and rebellious and will do anything to ruin your Kingdom effectiveness. The devil knows that the best way to hinder your effectiveness is to work against your new relationship with Christ. Deal ruthlessly with Satan! Renounce his work. Remove his opportunities to hurt you, and start anew! Jesus said, "The kingdom of heaven has been forcefully advancing, and forceful men lay hold of it" (Matt. 11:12, *NIV*).

If you will put into practice the principles we have written in this book, we are "confident of this very thing, that He who has begun a good work in you will complete it until the day of Jesus Christ" (Phil. 1:6). Blessings.

PRAYER ASSIGNMENT

Lord, thank You that what You have begun in me You will complete. I receive Your freedom and I will walk in the victory You've given to me in obedience to You.

I love You, Jesus. Amen!

Notes

1. Finis Jennings Dake, *Dake's Annotated Reference Bible*, as referenced from Exodus 13:2 (Lawrenceville, GA: Dake Bible Sales, 1963), p. 77.
2. Cindy Jacobs, *The Voice of God* (Ventura, CA: Regal Books, 1995), p. 241.
3. Ralph Woodrow, *Babylon Mystery Religion* (Riverside, CA: Ralph Woodrow Evangelistic Association, Inc., 1966), p. 10.

PERSONAL REVIEW

- What is in your home today?
- Has God shown you one or more possessions in your home that He now wants you to be rid of?
- Are there relationships in your life that dishonor God? What about past relationships? Are you willing to repent and stop these associations?
- Will you turn your heart to hear what He is saying concerning your life, your home and your possessions? Will you obey Him at all cost?
- What about ownership? Isn't it time to release ownership of your life and possessions to Him?
- Have you experienced the cleansing of your home and noticed a positive change in the spiritual environment?

We rejoice with you as you consider these action points and then do what you need to do to gain your freedom. Help others to learn the truth!

APPENDIX B

RECOMMENDED RESOURCES

Jackson, John Paul. *Buying and Selling the Souls of Our Children, A Closer Look at Pokemon.* N. Sutton, NH: Streams Publications, 2000.

Jacobs, Cindy. *Deliver Us from Evil.* Ventura, CA: Regal Books, 2001.

Prince, Derek. *They Shall Expel Demons.* Grand Rapids, MI: Chosen Books, 1998.

Smith, Alice. *Discerning the Climate of the City.* Houston, TX: SpiriTruth Publishing Co., 1997. (800) 569-4825.

_____. *Dispelling the Darkness.* Houston, TX: SpiriTruth Publishing Co., 1998. (800) 569-4825.

Smith, Eddie. *Ten Steps to Freedom.* Houston, TX: SpiriTruth Publishing Co., 1997. (800) 569-4825.

Wagner, C. Peter. *Confronting the Powers*. Ventura, CA: Regal Books, 1996.

_____. *Prayer Shield: How to Pray for Pastors*. Ventura, CA: Regal Books, 1992.

Wagner, Doris. *How to Cast Out Demons: A Guide to the Basics*. Ventura, CA: Regal Books, 2000.

Ministry Contact Page

Eddie and Alice Smith travel worldwide teaching on various themes related to revival and spiritual awakening. The Smiths teach together as well as individually on topics including prayer, intercession, deliverance, worship, spiritual warfare, spiritual mapping and Christian living.

For information about hosting the Smiths for a conference in your church or city, please check out their website at www.usprayercenter.org. When you click on Invite the Smiths, you will be shown an invitation form to complete and submit on-line. Or you can send a blank e-mail to request@usprayercenter.org. An auto-responder message will e-mail a speaker invitation form to you.

PRAYER RESOURCES

You can order Alice and Eddie's other books and materials, as well as resources they recommend, at www.prayerbookstore.com.

FREE NEWSLETTERS

PrayerNet
Alice Smith is senior editor of this FREE biweekly, informative Internet publication. Join thousands worldwide who receive *PrayerNet*. To subscribe, send a blank e-mail message to prayer net-subscribe@usprayercenter.org.

UpLink
Subscribe to Eddie and Alice's FREE inspiring, monthly postal publication *UpLink* (U.S. addresses only) by calling 713-466-4009 or 800-569-4825, or e-mail your name and mailing address to uplink@usprayercenter.org.

Eddie & Alice Smith
U.S. PRAYER CENTER
7710-T Cherry Park Dr., Ste. 224, Houston, TX 77095
Phone: (713) 466-4009; (800) 569-4825
Fax: (713) 466-5633
E-mail: usprayercenter@cs.com
Website: www.usprayercenter.org
Bookstore: www.prayerbookstore.com

GLOSSARY

aboriginal—the earliest inhabitants of a region.

Ai—a Canaanite city whose name literally means "a heap of ruins."

amulet—a charm used to ward off disease or evil spells.

angels—immortal spirit beings created by God to carry out His assignments; who operate in different levels of authority (see Eph. 6:12).

apparition—a ghostly figure.

Ark of the Covenant—a large rectangular wooden box overlaid with gold, upon which sat two angels with wings extended (protecting the articles inside), representing God's covenant with man.

artifact—an object produced or shaped by human craft, especially a tool, a weapon or an ornament of archaeological or historical interest.

Asherah poles—*See* **obelisks.**

astrology—the study of the positions and aspects of celestial bodies (through the use of the zodiac) based on the belief that the stars influence the course of human affairs.

Babel—the Hebrew name for Babylon, meaning "to confound."

Babylon—a city created by Nimrod, located in present-day Iraq; considered the seat of Satan, Scripture says it will ultimately be destroyed (see Rev. 14:8; 18).

Beelzebub—a name for Satan; also called the lord of the flies.

brass serpent—the symbol designed by God and made by Moses symbolizing man's insensibility and obstinacy in sin. It was elevated on a pole so that those bitten by poisonous serpents that had been sent as a punishment for their murmuring against God and against Moses could be healed (see Num. 21:4-9).

crescent moon—the figure of the moon as it appears in its first or last quarter, waxing (increasing) and waning (decreasing). It has concave and convex edges terminating in points and serves as one of the chief symbols of Islam.

crystal ball—a high-quality clear, colorless glass sphere used by mediums to portend the future.

curses—a calling down of evil or misfortune on someone or something (includes hexes, spells, etc.).

defile—to make unclean, to desecrate or pollute.

deliverance—(exorcism) to expel an evil spirit by command or prayer.

demon—an evil supernatural being; a devil.

demon possession—not mentioned in Scripture; Scripture uses the word"demonized," which means to be moved upon or within by an unclean spirit or spirits.

demonized—*See* **demon possession.**

devil—the archangel cast from heaven for leading the revolt of the angels; Satan; the personification of evil and the archenemy of God. Also used to refer to a subordinate evil spirit.

divination—foretelling future events or discovering things using magical powers.

dragon—a spiritual entity described as a gigantic reptile having a lion's claws, the tail of a serpent, wings and scaly skin; a symbol of Satan.

Egyptian ankh—the cross with a loop on top; represents a sex goddess who despises virginity; also a symbol promoting fertility rights, worshiping Ra the Egyptian sun god (Lucifer).

fallen angels—*See* **demon.**

familiar spirit—a demon that communicates with mediums (psychics), those who claim to consult with the dead; a spirit that operates within a family.

fetish—an object which is used to vex the environment with magic powers.

gargoyles—grotesque ornamental architectural figures found on old buildings; they were believed to ward off evil spirits.

geomancy—an Asian system of designing and arranging one's life according to blending of geometry and spiritism, involving some of the theories held by freemasonry.

ghosts—demonic apparitions disguising themselves as spirits of the dead.

heathen—one who adheres to the religion of a people or nation that does not acknowledge the God of Judaism and Christianity.

incantation—a formula of words used to produce magical or supernatural effects; the singing of a spell.

martial arts—any of several Asian arts of combat or self-defense, such as aikido, karate, judo or tae kwon do, based upon heathen deities, usually practiced as sport.

metaphysical—philosophies concerning realities beyond the physical, i.e., spiritual.

Mohammedans, Muslims—adherents of Islam, a monotheistic religion characterized by submission to the demonic god Allah and to Mohammed, his chief and last prophet.

multiple personality disorder—The misguided psychiatric diagnosis of the demonic, suggesting that in trauma the human soul splinters into multiple personalities which must be identified, befriended and merged together into one healthy personality.

Native American—a member of any of the aboriginal peoples of the Western Hemisphere whose ancestors are generally believed to have entered the Americas from Asia by way of the Bering Strait sometime during the late glacial epoch. Also called American Indian, Amerindian and Indian.

necromancy—the practice of supposedly communicating with the spirits of the dead in order to predict the future.

New Age—an amalgamation of metaphysical, naturalistic and spiritualist philosophies which call upon spiritual power apart from God.

obelisk—a tall, four-sided shaft of stone, with a pyramid-shaped point. It first appeared in the form of the Asherah pole, used in the worship of Baal and forbidden by God in the Old Testament. It was Asherah (or obelisk) that so infuriated God that He revealed Himself as jealous. (See Exod. 34:13-14; 1 Kings 14:15; 15:13.) It comes from the Hebrew word "asher" which means to erect. It is a symbol of the male phallic and refers to the earth's copulating with the sun. It is a favorite marking stone of Freemasonry. The Washington Monument is the most recognizable obelisk in the United States. It was completed in 1884 and is the tallest masonry structure in the world.

pentagram—a five-pointed star used as a magic symbol.

poltergeist—a noisy usually mischievous ghost held to be responsible for unexplained noises (as rappings).

possession—*See* **demon possession.**

rosary beads—a string of beads used for counting prayers in Catholicism; similar prayer beads are also used by other religious groups.

Satan—*See* **devil.**

Scientology—a rationalistic religion founded by American L. Ron Hubbard; this belief system emphasizes the healing of mind and body by means of following certain rules.

Septuagint—a Greek translation of the Old Testament (c. 300 B.C.).

shaman—an occult priest or witch doctor who uses magic to summon demonic power.

sorcerer—one who seeks to cast spells through incantations, to manipulate spirits or to practice black magic.

soul tie—a spiritual alliance between people that exerts supernatural control over them.

spiritual atmosphere—the prevailing spiritual presence in a region.

stronghold—a fortified place or a fortress.

strongman—the demonic ruler of a stronghold (see Matt. 12:29).

superstition—an irrational belief that an object, action or circumstance not logically related to a course of events influences its outcome.

talisman—an object or charm believed to confer supernatural powers, good luck or protection on its wearer.

unholy alliance—*See* **soul tie.**

Unity Church—a religious group that adheres to the doctrine of universal salvation regardless of the beliefs about the death and resurrection of Jesus.

witch—one who seeks supernatural power by practicing sorcery and enlisting the aid of demonic spirits.

witch doctor—an occult priest or shaman who summons demonic power to achieve some particular end.

word of knowledge—a spiritual gift, a manifestation of the Holy Spirit; to possess this gift is to know something beyond natural means through God's revelation (see 1 Cor. 12:8).

worry beads—a string of beads which the wearer fingers as a form of relaxation or distraction.

vex—to seek to confuse someone by means of a curse.

yoga—a Hindu discipline that seeks to train the consciousness to find a state of perfect spiritual insight and tranquillity.

zodiac—a celestial chart representing the paths of the principal planets of our solar system, it is the basis of astrology and is not related to the legitimate study of astronomy. Bottom line: The zodiac, a chart on which all astrology is based, has nothing at all to do with the actual locations of the stars and planets.